The Disci[

The Prophecies of Isaiah

A Call to Repentance

A Theological Exegesis by Dr. John W. (Jack) Carter

חזון ישעיהו
בן־אמוץ אשר חזה
על־יהודה וירושלם
בימי עזיהו יותם
אחז יחזקיהו מלכי
יהודה:

A publication of

The American Journal of Biblical Theology

Illuminating God's Word

www.biblicaltheology.com

Copyright © 2018, Dr. John W. (Jack) Carter

All rights reserved.

ISSN 1531-7919 (On-Line)
ISBN 9781981092567 (Paperback)

Table of Contents

Isaiah 1:1-20.	*The Apostate: A Church of Rebels*	Page	5
Isaiah 5:1-14	*The Fruitless Vinyard*		23
Isaiah 6:1-8	*Here Am I, LORD, Send Me!*		38
Isaiah 7:1-16.	*Trust the Good News of God*		54
Isaiah 17:1-14	*All Are Accountable*		67
Isaiah 28:14-22	*Where Do You Place Your Trust?*		77
Isaiah 30:12-18…	*Rejecting the Potter's Hand*		89
Isaiah 37:1-38	*Give Your Burdens to the LORD*		100
Isaiah 38:1-8;39:1-8	*The Folly of Human Choice*		121
Isaiah 40:1-14	*Comfort in Times of Trouble*		132
Isaiah 42:1-7	*God's Missionary Plan*		147
Isaiah 44:1-22	*Who (or What) Is Your God?*		160
Isaiah 45:1-13	*God Works Through His People*		173
Isaiah 53:1-12	*Prophecies of the Messiah*		182
Isaiah 55:1-13	*Priceless Grace*		197
Isaiah 58:1-14	*Time Out!*		211
Bibliography			226

Isaiah 1:1-20.
The Apostate: a Church of Rebels

```
YAZOwZ 1YIH
4w⟨ rYw⟨.19
A⟨YAZ.6O AIH
ZwZ9 wGwY4ZY
wXYZ YAZIO
YAZ⌽IHZ IH⟨
A⟨YAZ Z⋎Gw [1]
```

When one thinks of the church, one envisions a body of believers who have put their faith and trust in God. The Lord of the Church is God. Under His Lordship, the church is a family of brothers and sisters under one loving and guiding Father. God has commissioned the church to spread the good news of His love and His grace to all the world, for it is His will that all the world would be saved. With the Holy Spirit empowering the hearts of each believer, they are motivated to actions that demonstrate God's love among themselves, in their

---
[1] Isaiah 1:1. Paleo-Hebrew (before 585 B.C.)

community, and throughout the world as they are fully engaged in the work of ministry. There are many churches today that can be described by this model as they are led by Godly men and women who love the Lord and facilitate others to follow. God seems to have planted his faithful remnant in many communities around the world, and their ministries of prayer and action make a true and meaningful impact for the work of God's kingdom on earth.

For a church to be so characterized, it has only one option among two mutually-exclusive choices: obedience to God rather than obedience to this pagan and secular culture. What happens when a church succumbs to the secular messages of this pagan world? What happens when the true desire of the church is to be accepted by the world rather than be accepted by God? I am reminded of a main-stream denomination church in California that voted to remove all prayer and all mention of God from its worship services so that no person would be "offended." Considering the Bible to be offensive to some, a women's Bible study group was told to choose between disbanding or leaving the church when some began sharing testimonies of salvation. This is a church that wanted to be accepted by its community so much that it chose to discard all matters of faith and godliness. The result is a large social club that has a Christian theme, attempting to present the form of religion, but contains none of its substance. Though this is an extreme example, this same spirit can pervade a congregation in far more subtle ways as the Lordship of God is replaced by the Lordship of individuals or small groups who wish to control the body. The purpose, mission, and work of these churches is shaped by the personal agendas of self-centered individuals rather than by the Holy Spirit. They may "look" like a church, but own little or none of its power as it is simply another secular social club with its own rules of membership and behavior that serves to exclude others who do not conform to the desires of its leadership.

In observing these church cultures, we have identified two ends of a spectrum, where at one end we find a body who is immersed in their love for God, and at the other end a body who is immersed in their love for this world. All of us stand somewhere on this spectrum, and hopefully all who understand the context of faith are seeking to move along that line closer and closer to God. It is for this very purpose that God has revealed Himself to man, so that we would know Him and turn to Him in faith, and by so doing receiving from Him forgiveness for our sins that serve only to separate us from Him.

We see in the history of ancient Israel the consequence that is realized when the church seeks to be worldly instead of Godly. God revealed Himself in a very personal way to Abraham, making him a promise that his faith would be rewarded in a multitude of ways: (1) Abraham and Sarah would have a son in their advanced years, (2) through this son would rise a mighty nation, (3) God would give him and his nation both the land and the protection to live in it as long as they were obedient to Him, and (4) through his seed the entire world would be blessed. Note that the maintenance of that third promise was predicated upon obedience. It is God's expectation that the church will embrace Him as their Lord.

Following the years of the faithfulness of Abraham, Isaac, Jacob, and Joseph, the nation grew as it was kept in isolation by the Egyptian Pharaohs. Subjected to continual persecution and bondage in Egypt, God miraculously returned them to the promised land in Canaan in the Exodus that is so well known in history. Prior to entering the promised land, God made another covenant with the people at Mt. Sinai through Moses, a covenant that restated God's promise to give them land and protection as long as they would be obedient to Him. The people agreed that they would be "His people," and He would be "their God." However, though there was always a small remnant of faithful in the body, the preponderant majority of the nation of Israel failed to be obedient to God, instead choosing to follow the sensual and secular pagan religions of the Canaanites. After about 400 years among the Canaanites, their desire to "be like the nations" led them to desire a king rather than the Lord, and God gave them Saul, David, and Solomon who together reigned for about 120 years. David's son, Solomon placed the people of Israel in bondage to his building campaigns, and his son Rehoboam, in his declaration of further bondage split the nation in 917 B.C. He retained the southern kingdom of Judah while the other tribes of Jacob broke away and formed the northern kingdom of Israel.

During the entire history of the northern kingdom none of its kings led the nation to follow God, but rather, became involved in international intrigue, becoming a pawn in the wars among their embattled neighbors. The southern kingdom of Judah contained the remnant of faithful who occasionally included its kings. It is into this period of history that the prophet Isaiah is born.

> **Isaiah 1:1.** *The vision of Isaiah the son of Amoz, which he saw concerning Judah and Jerusalem in the days of Uzziah, Jotham, Ahaz, and Hezekiah, kings of Judah.*

The lack of a calendar system we use today, historical documents were often identified in reference to the years of the reign of kings. When we compare such historical documents is its a relatively easy process to map those years onto the modern calendar. We find that Isaiah ministered during the years of king Uzziah through Hezekiah, and presumably lived to witness the reign of Manasseh, the godless king who followed Hezekiah. The period of history chronicled by Isaiah is also recorded in 2 Kings 15-21, and 2 Chronicles 26-33. These Old Testament books, as well as many non-canonical writings in history, genealogy, and literature serve to corroborate the life and times of Isaiah. Consequently, the teachings and prophesies of Isaiah are quoted more frequently in scripture than all of the other prophets combined.

We have no scriptural documentation to identify Amoz, though Jewish traditional literature holds that he was a brother of one of Israel's kings, placing him and his family in Jerusalem, and close to the throne. This is certainly consistent with Isaiah's location in Jerusalem and the close association he had with its kings. Isaiah served God during the most turbulent years of Israel's history. Since breaking away as a nation, Israel never served God. God's promise to give them the land was predicated on their obedience, and 20 years into Isaiah's ministry, Israel was obliterated by the Assyrians in 722B.C., with about 30,000 of its people taken captive and the remainder scattered among foreigners who were brought in with the purpose of dissolving Jewish culture. Apostasy refers to the state of rejecting God in favor of the things of this world. Recognizing Israel's apostasy, Isaiah prophesied to Israel for that period of 20 years, calling them back to obedience to God. At the same time, the southern nation of Judah was also falling away from God and embracing the secular and pagan culture, so Isaiah continued to prophesy to Judah until his death, presumably at the hands of Manasseh.

We find in Isaiah's writings the voice of God as he spoke to apostate Israel, to Judah whose population, other than the remnant of faithful, were also falling into apostasy and would face the same demise. Consequently, we hear the voice of God to the church today, a church that is in many ways similar to Judah, a church that contains a remnant of faithful, but also a large body of those who seek to follow the culture of the world.

Finally, we find in the writings of Isaiah the voice of God as He spoke a message of hope for the remnant, a promise that the Messiah would come, a Messiah who would would suffer at the hands of evil men to save the faithful from the curse of sin that separates them from God, a Messiah who would be Jesus.

> **Isaiah 1:2.** *Hear, O heavens, and give ear, O earth: for the LORD hath spoken, I have nourished and brought up children, and they have rebelled against me.*

The context and content of Isaiah's vision from God is immediately apparent. God equates the apostasy of Israel (including Judah) with rebellion. God has been faithful to His promise to Abraham. He protected them as a nation in Egypt, brought them to the promised land, and protected them as the nation grew. God provided for their needs in the wilderness, and brought them to a land that was fertile and already planted. Never in the history of mankind did people so frequently see the hand of God as they experienced miracle after miracle that each served to protect them and validate the power of God to do so. The people also witnessed the continual presence of the Glory of God as it stood over the tabernacle. As the nation of Israel was forming in the land of promise, it was as close to God as a child is to a loving parent. The opportunities for Israel were limitless. However, Isaiah summarizes the state of Israel, the children of God, in one simple word: rebellion.

Many parents have experienced the rebellion of a child, when that child turns his/her back on the parent, rejecting their love and their hopes, seeking to find their needs met from another source. The rebellion of a child is a good metaphor for apostasy. As the child rebels against the parent and seeks out his/her own entrance into the world, the nation of Israel rebelled against God's authority, denying the covenant made at Mt. Sinai, and chose to become immersed in the secular and pagan culture. Though they wore the garments of the temple, they lived the life of the pagan. They looked religious, talked with religious words, and held to religion's piety, but in their hearts and actions they were fully immersed in godlessness. They assumed that they were righteous by association, simply because they were "children of God," yet they lived lives that were fully secular. Instead of worshipping God, they bowed to the pagan gods and took part in pagan practices that were unlimited in their sinfulness. Their rebellion against God was so complete that God had placed in motion the circumstances that would result in the removal of his hand of protection from them, and they would ultimately lose the land of promise.

At the beginning of Isaiah's ministry, neither nation had yet experienced the removal of God's hand of protection. Israel was not at all concerned about any need for such protection, and Judah thought it was invincible because of God's presence in the Jerusalem temple. While Amos and Hosea would prophesy to Israel in the north, seeking to bring Israel back to God, Isaiah and Micah would prophesy to Judah in the south, warning them of their same need. The children of God have rebelled against their father, and all of the heavens and earth need to hear this message.

> **Isaiah 1:3.** *The ox knoweth his owner, and the ass his master's crib: but Israel doth not know, my people doth not consider.*

When God looks at the rebellion of the people he contrasts their ignorance with the faithfulness of the dumbest of animals.

Certainly the ox is not as intelligent as a human being, yet even the ox is faithful to its owner. The ox responds to its owner's voice as it works for him. The ox knows where its food comes from and recognizes the reward of it for obedient behavior. Likewise, the ass knows where its home is: in the crib of his master. Left to wander, or if engaged in labor, the ass returns to his own master's crib where it receives food and shelter from the master's hand. If even the dumbest of animals can recognize to whom they belong and the source of their sustenance, how much more should people not recognize the same? Yet, in their rebellion, the people do not know their master, and do not give consideration as to the source of their sustenance. We can still see this pattern today. People love their pet animals who are uncompromising in their faithfulness to their master, yet at the same time they either declare that there is no God, or at least demonstrate such a belief in their actions. Like the children of Israel, they chase after this secular culture, embracing its euphemisms, and rationalizing away their own ungodly attitudes and behaviors. When those who call themselves Christians fall into this pattern, they become like the nation of Judah and the message that Isaiah brings against this rebellious nation becomes just as relevant for the church today. It is quite a contrast that unintelligent animals so easily know faithfulness, yet people find it so elusive.

> **Isaiah 1:4.** *Ah sinful nation, a people laden with iniquity, a seed of evildoers, children that are corrupters: they have forsaken the LORD, they have provoked the Holy One of Israel unto anger, they are gone away backward.*

The sinfulness of Israel and Judah cannot be understated, and their rebellion against God does not come without consequence. Isaiah characterizes the nation in four ways. As a nation, it does not stand for God as it was called to do. Instead, both nations followed their godless kings into deals with their warring neighbors, deals that pitted them against the nations that God called them to open to Him. The people are laden with iniquity. The image is that of an animal bending under a burden, as the people are overpowered by the burden of their own sin. The sinfulness of the people only serves to enable the wicked, bringing them to positions of power and influence. As a result, the governments of both Israel and Judah are evil and corrupt. Corruption breeds corruption, and such evil overpowers good when that which is good finds no defenders. Corruption stands against the goodness of God, and a corrupt Israel stands condemned of treason against the God who formed it as a nation. The pagan nations do not stand in such judgment, since they have been pagan from the beginning. It was Israel's task to take God to the pagan nations. Instead they have abandoned God in order to be like the pagan nations.

God is a Holy God, and in order to maintain His Holiness He cannot condone any measure of sin. Consequently, there is a consequence to Israel's apostasy: God's anger. God must deal with Israel's sin, or God is not God. Likewise, God must deal with our own sin as He exercises His sovereignty. Biblical prophesies frequently describe the anger of God as being provoked by the sinfulness of man. The destruction of mankind in the flood of Noah's generation and the destruction of Sodom and Gomorrah are examples of the consequence of God's provocation. Can God again demonstrate His anger towards the sinfulness of man with similar events of destruction?

> **Isaiah 1:5-6.** *Why should ye be stricken any more? ye will revolt more and more: the whole head is sick, and the whole heart faint. ⁶From*

> *the sole of the foot even unto the head there is no soundness in it; but wounds, and bruises, and putrifying sores: they have not been closed, neither bound up, neither mollified with ointment.*

The consequences of sin go far deeper then an event of final destruction. Sin brings a destruction that is slow and painful. God promised both the land and protection to His children simply in exchange for their obedience. When we turn our back on God we, like the ancient Israelites, step out from under that hand of protection the God promises, and the consequences of our choices can be epic. It is God's will that no person should suffer the consequence of separation from Himself, yet God allows us to make choices that are clearly not in our own best interests, choices that do bring suffering upon ourselves. God describes the state of apostate Israel like that of a body which is stricken with a mortal sickness. Every act of rebellion only serves to stricken the body with additional sickness, weakness, wounds, bruises, and sores. Without God there is no source of healing for this insidious decay. Without God there is simply no hope. Why would anyone choose such suffering? Why do we prefer to experience the consequence of sin rather than simply trust in God?

> **Isaiah 1:7.** *Your country is desolate, your cities are burned with fire: your land, strangers devour it in your presence, and it is desolate, as overthrown by strangers.*

Just as the children of God are individually called to obedience, so is their nation. The consequences of sin that are realized by individuals are also realized by the nation from which they are formed. A godless people will form a godless nation, a nation that is likewise outside of God's hand of protection, exposed to the ravages of sin's consequences. Both Israel and Judah have already experienced the consequence of their apostasy as God's hand of protection has been lifted. Thinking of themselves as a pair of mighty nations, both Israel and Judah were simply annoyances to their far superior neighbors. Rather than seeking protection in the arms of God, their godless kings chose alliances among their larger, warring neighbors, and by so doing entering into their continual conflicts as each of the larger nations were continually bent on conquest. As a result, both nations found themselves with a tenuous and dangerous friend on one side, and a deadly enemy on the other. Continued military skirmishes resulted in the destruction of most of their smaller cities as the conquests of their neighbors continually included their own people and land.

When we step out from under God's protection, we enter a dangerous land. Depending upon ourselves for our own security, we are subject to far greater powers that would defeat us. Why is it that we are so astonished when we suffer defeat? Why do we blame God for our own demise? Rebellion against God is our own choice, and as we are free to make that choice, we are also free to suffer the consequences.

> **Isaiah 1:8.** *And the daughter of Zion is left as a cottage in a vineyard, as a lodge in a garden of cucumbers, as a besieged city.*

The state of the people and the state of the nation are also mirrored in the state of Jerusalem: exposed by their choice of abandoning God's hand of protection. The picture painted here is one that fits the context of the feudal kingdom structure. Kings lived in walled cities, and during times of siege, the people in the surrounding communities would run to the protection provided by the city walls, leaving their cottages and loges exposed. The vineyard is not going to slow the invading army's advance on the cottage any more than the garden of cucumbers will protect the farmer's lodge. When we rebel against God, and choose to step outside of his hand of protection, we step outside of the fortified walls, placing our trust in the grapevines and cucumbers to stop the power of the advancing army. is it any wonder that so many people are so defeated? Is it any wonder that even those who call themselves Christians fail to experience victory in their lives, as they are buffeted by every passing storm?

> **Isaiah 1:9.** *Except the LORD of hosts had left unto us a very small remnant, we should have been as Sodom, and we should have been like unto Gomorrah.*

There was one very significant difference between the state of the pagan nations, the state of Israel, and the state of Judah: the remnant. The pagan nations had no remnant of faithful believers, so they were not guilty of apostasy. They were, and are, simply lost and in need of the knowledge of God's grace. The kingdom of Israel contained almost no remnant at all. Since Amos and Hosea prophesied there, we know that a remnant remained, but we find no indication of their influence in any of the nation's history. Furthermore, we find no evidence of the miraculous protection of that remnant when Israel was destroyed by the Assyrians. However, we do know that refugees from the north fled to Judah, and this certainly could have included the remnant. The remnant of Judah was substantially larger, and as a nation, Judah survived for over 100 years following the destruction of Israel. When Judah was destroyed by Babylon, its king Nebuchadnezzar took the remnant captive, protecting them from the subsequent annihilation of the remainder of the kingdom. God always kept his promise to protect those who were faithful to Him, and as Isaiah repeats God's word, he notes that it is the remnant that has kept Israel and Judah from suffering the same demise as both Sodom and Gomorrah, cities that were destroyed by God during the lifetime of Abraham and his nephew, Lot, cities that demonstrated a clear lack of any remnant of faithful people. The demise of Sodom and Gomorrah were examples of God's wrath against a community that contained no remnant.

How much of our world today is protected against utter destruction because of the existence of a remnant of faithful believers?

> **Isaiah 1:10-14.** *Hear the word of the LORD, ye rulers of Sodom; give ear unto the law of our God, ye people of Gomorrah. [11]To what purpose is the multitude of your sacrifices unto me? saith the LORD: I am full of the burnt offerings of rams, and the fat of fed beasts; and I delight not in the blood of bullocks, or of lambs, or of he goats. [12]When ye come to appear before me, who hath required this at your hand, to tread my courts? [13]Bring no more vain oblations; incense is an abomination unto me; the new moons and sabbaths, the calling of assemblies, I cannot away with; it is iniquity, even the solemn meeting. [14]Your new moons and your appointed feasts my soul hateth: they are a trouble unto me; I am weary to bear them.*

As Isaiah continues, he speaks to the faithless of the city, both its leaders and its citizens. As we consider the state of ancient Israel and Judah, we must always keep one truth in mind: These were a very religious people. If you were to walk down the streets of Jerusalem, you would find yourself surrounded by the appearance of religious piety. After all, these were the children of God, the chosen people. They defined themselves by (1) their descent from Abraham, and (2) by the presence of God in the temple. They wore religious clothing that conformed with the Law and with their traditions. The leaders of the city as well as its inhabitants looked religious and pious, and they were convinced of their own righteousness because of it. They continued to burn the traditional sacrifices, but God refused to accept them. We may remember Adam's sacrifice that came from the heart, and Cain's sacrifice that came from arrogance and contempt. God accepted the former, and rejected the latter. We did not learn from this lesson. Though they rejected God in their hearts, they maintained the hypocrisy of their traditions, continuing in their celebration of holidays and feasts, events that became objects of their own consumptions and lusts rather than days that were spent honoring God and remembering what He had done for them. God is not impressed with vain sacrifice.

> **Isaiah 1:10-15.** *And when ye spread forth your hands, I will hide mine eyes from you: yea, when ye make many prayers, I will not hear: your hands are full of blood.*

Among all of these verses, this statement is arguably the most pointed, serving as the fulcrum of this passage: God does not even receive their worship. Though they lift their hands and shout praises, though they fall prostrate to the ground and recite many prayers, their hypocrisy is known to God. Their worship is simply a show for one another, a testimony among themselves of how religious and pious they are. This is a worship that is permeated by self-centered pride rather than by a genuine love for God. Just as God rejects the sacrifices, offerings, and holidays, he rejects the worship of those who do so only for show. The Jews invested about 800 years in these traditions, and were so well-ingrained in them that they were able to perpetuate them for yet another 400 years without giving consideration to their purpose of worship.

How much of today's worship is done in vain? When we come together to worship, do we worship God, or do we follow a traditional process of behaviors while we continue to worship only ourselves? If God rejects the worship of those who are not truly worshipping Him, will he reject our worship? God will not hear when our hands are full of blood: when we stand before Him condemned by Him of our sin, sin that we will not even acknowledge ourselves. For the Jews, this blood was in many ways quite literal as they had on their own hands the blood of those whom they killed, those who criticized their godless tradition and called upon the people to turn to God. The propensity for the Jews to kill the leadership of the remnant was universal: their persecution of the prophets continued through the crucifixion of the Messiah at Calvary.

The Christian church cannot stand in arrogance and piety on this issue. We have seen throughout history how the organized Christian church followed this same pattern, particularly in the dark ages when those who criticized the church were frequently persecuted and burned at the stake. Though the organized church may not be as apt to kill its critics as it did in the past, it still has the means and purpose to persecute those who would challenge it. God was not the central authority of Israel or Judah, and too often, God is not the central authority of the church. Like the ancient Jews we may continue to wear the religious clothes, speak religious words, and recite an endless litany of pious prayers. However, it is not the clothes, words, or prayers that honor God: it is only the heart that honors God. When those clothes, words, and prayers are offered to God as a genuine act of worship of a beloved God, that worship is received. Paul notes in the 12th chapter of his letter to the Romans how God accepts the worship of people when i t comes from their heart, without regard to the content that characterize that worship.

> **Isaiah 1:16-18.** *Wash you, make you clean; put away the evil of your doings from before mine eyes; cease to do evil; ^{17}Learn to do well; seek judgment, relieve the oppressed, judge the fatherless, plead for the widow. ^{18}Come now, and let us reason together, saith the LORD: though your sins be as scarlet, they shall be as white as snow; though they be red like crimson, they shall be as wool.*

Up to this point, the state of Israel and Judah looks quite hopeless. Likewise, the state of the modern church that has also rebelled against God looks similarly hopeless. However, God has always been a God of new beginnings. God always offers forgiveness for those who will repent of their sin and turn to Him in faith and trust. It is amazing that God has watched the children of Israel immerse themselves in apostasy for, at this point, 700 years, and yet His offer of forgiveness still stands. Can the people turn from their wicked ways and accept God's offer of forgiveness. When called upon to become washed, the religious Jews answer, "we are clean." When called upon to put away their evil, they answer, "we have done no evil." When called upon to learn to do well, they reply "we keep the law," when called upon to seek judgment they reply "our courts offer sound judgment," when called upon to relieve the oppressed they reply, "there is no one who is oppressed who does not deserve it," when called upon to rightly judge the fatherless they reply, "they are bastards, they do not deserve to be treated like I should be treated;" their response to the widow is similar. Yet, they maintain their piousness and self-declared righteousness. Though this is an apt description of the religious leaders in ancient Israel, is there a thread of such attitudes in religious leadership today?

Again, God offers forgiveness. To those who will put away such prideful and self-centered attitudes and turn to Him in faith and trust, God offers complete forgiveness, a completely new start. As bad as one's sins may have been, God will forgive them entirely, holding us accountable only for our love for Him and not for what we have done in the past.

> **Isaiah 1:19-20.** *If ye be willing and obedient, ye shall eat the good of the land: [20]But if ye refuse and rebel, ye shall be devoured with the sword: for the mouth of the LORD hath spoken it.*

God's covenant offer to Israel is the same covenant offer that He made with them 700 years ago at the foot of Mt. Sinai: if you will be obedient, you will receive the land and the hand of God's protection. However, if you refuse and rebel against God, you will step outside of that hand of protection, you will lose the land, and you will be devoured by the sin of this wicked world.

The choice given to Israel is the same choice given to people today. God offers blessing and protection to those who will place their faith and trust in Him. When we refuse to place our trust in God, we make the choice to reject that offer of blessing and protection, depending upon ourselves to survive in this wicked world, and depending upon ourselves for our own salvation. Satan may lead us to believe that we can do these things on our own, but any form of true reason (vs. 18) reveals the inefficacy of such a choice. To reject God's offer of blessing and protection, as well as God's offer for salvation from the eternal consequence of our sin is in itself an act of self-destructive foolishness.

This is not the end ... it is only the introduction to the prophecy of Isaiah. As we read through this lengthy oracle, we will experience the demise of the northern nation of Israel and the dissolution of the southern nation of Judah through the eyes of the prophet. Isaiah exposes the signs and judgments that are illustrated in historic events. Isaiah exposes at great length the consequences of the rebellion, not only of Israel and Judah, but that of the surrounding nations who by attacking Israel are in their own hearts attacking their God, declaring themselves as the enemies of the Lord Most High. Isaiah continually exposes the various sins of the nations and calls upon them to repent and turn to God, warning them of the coming judgment that will take the form of the destruction of the kingdoms. As Isaiah presents his prophecy against the wickedness of Israel and Judah, he never fails to weave through that message the offer of forgiveness and restoration to those who will repent and turn to God.

When we look at the southern nation of Judah, and use reason to compare it with the church today, we will find many parallels. Both groups are convinced of their own righteousness, yet both groups exhibit a bent to worldliness and sin. Consequently, the prophecy of Isaiah to Judah is just as relevant for the church today. So stand in rebellion against God is to take ourselves out from under his hand of protection, and the experience of both Israel and Judah is an example for us today, that we would not make the same mistakes and suffer the same fate, but that we would put down our arrogance and pride and return to God that which He truly deserves: His Lordship over us and over the body of believers, His church.

Isaiah 5:1-14.
The Fruitless Vinyard

God has a plan and purpose for His creation: that through it He would be glorified. It would be through creation that God would form man in His image, and call man to Himself that we might find a relationship with Him. When we observe the creation event as narrated in the book of Genesis, we find that God referred to His creation as "good."[2] However, that goodness was shattered when sin entered the world through the self-centered choices of man, choices that entered man's

---

[2] Genesis 1:4,10,12,18,21,25,31, et. al.

thoughts and actions through the influence of the evil one[3] who, in rebellion against God, seeks to turn this world away from God and to himself.

If we consider that God created a Garden of Eden, a place of beauty and innocence where God walked with man, what do we find when we look at the world around us. What happened? Where is the innocence of Adam and Eve that existed before the fall? Is it lost forever? When we look at the world today, what do we see? What went wrong?

God has been progressively revealing Himself and His purpose to mankind since the fall of man into sin and rebellion. He demonstrated man's arrogance and His sovereignty when He confounded man at the Tower of Babel.[4] Sin continued to run rampant in the world until He provided cleansing through the great flood.[5] God called the faithful man Abraham out of the ancestors of Noah to be the father of a nation whom God would draw to Himself as priests to the world, a nation that God would use to bless all other nations. This nation would become Israel, a people who, like Adam and Eve, rebelled against God's sovereignty and suffered the consequences of their sin. Isaiah wrote his prophecies during the waning years of the Jewish state. Isaiah's ministry started with the death of Judah's king Uzziah (740 B.C.) to approximately 690 B.C. It was during his ministry that the northern nation of Israel was destroyed and dispersed by Assyria (722 B.C.). Isaiah had watched the demise of the northern kingdom, and witnessed a similar dissolution of Judah, a downward spiral that would result in Judah's destruction only a few generations after Isaiah's death.

---

[3] Matthew 13:19,38; John 17:15, e.g.
[4] Genesis 11:19.
[5] Genesis 6:13, ff.

Isaiah's prophecy starts with a reminder of God's sovereignty, His purpose of creation, and His care for Israel. As Israel is falling away from God, Isaiah first calls for purity,[6] prophesies of Israel's coming peace and apostasy.[7]

Chapter 5 introduces an abrupt change in the format of Isaiah's writing as he changes from prose to poetry. Chapter 5 is a grand and complex poem that emotes both Isaiah's emotions and his understanding of God's purpose for Israel. Translating this form of writing presents particular challenges as it includes the added difficulty of determining the meaning behind abstract thoughts and images.

Isaiah's poem depicts the nation of Israel as a vineyard, a common scriptural metaphor,[8] one that he had already used in his description of the plundering of Israel by its neighbors.[9] The planting, maintenance, and harvesting of a vineyard was a well-understood task, providing Isaiah with a colorful means of presenting a message of God's purpose for His people as He planted the nation and provided the resources to bring it growth and fruition.

> **Isaiah 5:1.** *Now will I sing to my wellbeloved a song of my beloved touching his vineyard. My wellbeloved hath a vineyard in a very fruitful hill:*

Isaiah is going to present his message as a poem, one that he describes as being presented in song. Hebrew poetry rhymes ideas rather than sounds, so as we look at each phrase, it is

---

[6] Isaiah 1:1-31.
[7] Isaiah 2:1-4:6.
[8] Jeremiah 12:10, Ezekiel 19:10, Micah 1:6, Matthew 20:1, e.g.
[9] Isaiah 3:14.

appropriate to examine how each pairing of ideas develops a single thought.

Isaiah first notes his relationship with the owner of the vineyard, referring to the LORD as his Beloved. This speaks to the close and personal relationship that Isaiah had with God, a relationship that God desires for all people. It is through this relationship that the LORD was able to reveal His plan and purpose for Israel through Isaiah.

Then, Isaiah notes that the vineyard is planted on a very fertile hill. The arid country around the region of Israel made any fertile region to be notable. The phrase carries the connotation that the vineyard owner has planted His vineyard on very fertile soil. Because of the soil's fertility, the vineyard should be able to grow and flourish.

The vineyard is also placed on a hill. The word used for hill conveys the idea of a place that is visible to all. Like a city on a hill that cannot be hidden,[10] this vineyard, Israel, will be seen by all and known by all.

In some ways, the modern church is much like that vineyard that God has planted and has empowered with His Holy Spirit to grow and flourish. Likewise, the church is visible to all and serves as a testimony, positive or negative, to God's grace on earth.

> **Isaiah 5:2.** *And he fenced it, and gathered out the stones thereof, and planted it with the choicest vine, and built a tower in the midst of it, and also made a winepress therein: and he*

---

[10] Matthew 5:14-16.

looked that it should bring forth grapes, and it brought forth wild grapes.

The LORD of the vineyard put a tremendous amount of work into the preparation of the land for His vineyard. The word rendered "fencing" refers to the very difficult task of **breaking up of hard, dry, soil** for the first time. I am reminded of my first attempt to plant azaleas in the hard clay of the North Carolina Piedmont region. After a frustrating attempt to dig with a shovel, I tried to carve a hole in the ground with a hammer and screwdriver. I broke the screwdriver. This illustrates the toughness of the soil that God has to work with as He is preparing His people for His purpose of grace. The soil is greatly fertile, but it strongly resists the efforts of the LORD to plant the seed.

The Owner then **cleared the land of stones**. Stones serve as obstacles to the tiller that must be removed as part of the preparation of the land. We are quite hopeless without the power of God to prepare our hearts for Him when it is so filled with barriers. Isaiah describes God as the One who removes those barriers so that His work can be accomplished.

The Owner then planted the vineyard with the **choicest of vines**. There was (and still is) a wide variety of vines that one can plant in a vineyard. The ancient contemporaries of Isaiah would identify and understand well when the Owner is selecting the very choicest of vines. These vines would be out of the reach for the average farmer, being far too costly to obtain, and representing far too great a risk in this arid land where so many things can diminish the quality of the harvest. Farmers understand the faith that is necessary to plant a crop with an expectation of harvest. In this metaphor, the Owner is demonstrating great faith as He is prepared the land for the very best and most valuable harvest imaginable.

Even before the harvest, the Owner built a stone **watchtower** in the center of the vineyard. This tower would serve two important purposes. First, it would provide housing for the Owner. The concept is that the Owner will live in the midst of his vineyard, that He will be present with his crop during the period of its development through to the point of harvest. His presence also implies his responsiveness to serve the needs of the vineyard, providing it with His protection.

I vineyard does not produce a viable crop for a couple of years. However, the Owner immediately built the **winepress**, implying His confidence that the harvest will be fruitful.

The owner had put into place an optimum setting for the production of the finest grapes. He could look forward to a great and valuable crop, the finest crop in the lands. No typical farmer would go through all of what the Owner had done, and so His expectation could be greater than that of any farmer. However, we find that the crop did not produce as the Owner had intended. Instead of producing the finest of grapes, this vineyard produced only **wild grapes**. His vineyard produced disappointment. Wild grapevines produce few grapes, and those are dry and sour, not suitable for the production of good wine, and certainly not suitable for the production of fine wine.
Likewise, God has put in place all that is needed for His people to develop into people of faith who love Him and serve Him with a bounty of spiritual fruit. However, when sin entered the world, God could find only great disappointment. God created us and has a right to expect our faithful obedience. However, we have turned our backs on Him and chosen to live in this world, reaping a minimal and bitter harvest that this world produces.

> **Isaiah 5:3-4.** *And now, O inhabitants of Jerusalem, and men of Judah, judge, I pray you, betwixt me and my vineyard. ⁴What could have been done more to my vineyard, that I have not done in it? wherefore, when I looked that it should bring forth grapes, brought it forth wild grapes?*

We see in this parable a frustrated owner, as though he is scratching his head and asking the question, "What more could I have done?" What more could God do for man to provide him with every opportunity for a life that is faithful and full of spiritual fruit? God revealed Himself to all people through His Word and through His Creation. It is evident to all that there is one God, and that He is a righteous God. Furthermore, it is evident to all that we are unrighteous, and instead of producing the finest of fruits, we have chosen to lead self-serving lives with a bitter fruit like that of the wild grapes, rather than that of the choicest fruit that God deserves.

The fault in this parable does not lie in the owner, but rather in the vine itself. As the vine planted in fertile soil, we have chosen to bear the fruit of sin by choice. This apostasy certainly characterized the chosen nation of Israel who had promised faithfulness to God when it was delivered from Egypt, but turned away from Him to seek the sensual and accepted practices of their pagan neighbors. The church today shows signs of similar apostasy as it continues to accept as normative more and more egregious lifestyle sins. God's word provides a moral compass that much of the church has abandoned, following the pattern of ancient Israel. The good spiritual fruit that should be the product of the church is being replaced by the sour fruit of that wild grape.

What is the Vintner to do with a crop of useless, wild grapes? They are not suitable for his profit, and are not worthy of his continued cultivation and protection.

> **Isaiah 5:5-6.** *And now go to; I will tell you what I will do to my vineyard: I will take away the hedge thereof, and it shall be eaten up; and break down the wall thereof, and it shall be trodden down: ⁶And I will lay it waste: it shall not be pruned, nor digged; but there shall come up briers and thorns: I will also command the clouds that they rain no rain upon it.*

Though the Vintner prepared the soil, planted the seed, cultivated the vineyard, and provided continued protection of its vines, when it came to fruition it proved to be without worth. There is no point in investing any more resources in the preservation of a crop that is nothing more than weeds. How does the vintner respond to this circumstance?

1. **Remove the hedge of protection.** The hedge refers to the protection that the Vintner provided during the growing season. There is no longer any need to maintain this hedge, so by his lifting his hand of protection, the hedge will fall to the elements, allowing all manner of natural enemies to invade and destroy the vines. The beautiful vineyard on the hill will lose its definition, now blending in with the rest of the uncultivated hillside.
2. **The vine will be downtrodden.** The degradation of the hedge will allow passersby to simply walk through it and through the vineyard like so many other weeds, beating down both the hedge and the vines. The vine will be

walked on by its neighbors, trodden underfoot to its destruction.

3. **Lay to waste.** When God removes His hand of protection, the only result is a barren waste. God is not going to treat the vine as if it's a choice grape, even though it may think that it is. He will treat the vine as it truly deserves to be treated: left to its own devices. Without the Vintner's protection the lack of pruning will cause the vine to run wild and minimize the production of even its own sour fruit. Furthermore, the lack of cultivation that God would have provided will allow all manner of thorns and briers to intermingle with it. The vine will lose its identity, and be choked by the things of this world.

4. **Removal of sustenance.** Finally, the Vintner has no reason to expend the resources necessary to feed the vine. Without life-giving water, the vine will only wither and die. The life of the vineyard is now short, lasting only a single season.

God had intended that His vineyard would produce good fruit, and that He would sustain it forever. However, instead of bearing good fruit, it turned wild and bore the fruit of a wild plant, serving no good purpose of the LORD.

Isaiah's readers would understand this parable. They would agree that the investment that the Vintner initially made could only have been considered a total loss, and the land that was given to the vineyard is now without value.

> **Isaiah 5:7.** *For the vineyard of the LORD of hosts is the house of Israel, and the men of Judah his pleasant plant: and he looked for judgment, but behold oppression; for righteousness, but behold a cry.*

If there is any doubt that this parable was intended to expose the state of the nation of Israel, Isaiah moves to remove it at this point. The vineyard represents the current state of Israel, God's chosen nation. God prepared Israel as a choice vineyard, giving it the opportunity to produce a fruit like the world has never seen. God revealed Himself and His word to the children of Abraham, giving them instruction on obedience. Had they turned to Him in faith, they would have served as a nation of priests. They would have dispensed God's judgment throughout the land, a judgment that has at its foundation the very love of God. However, Israel chose rebellion against God, and produced only oppression. Rather than minister to the needy, they condemn and brutalize them. Rather than demonstrate the righteousness of God, they are characterized by sin and strife. Rather than hear the praises of the people, God hears their cries of suffering. This was not the purpose or intent that God had for Israel. It is simply the purpose and intent that was the product of Israel's choice to disregard faith in God and replace it with faith in the things of this world, the wild briar-patch that provides no true and lasting resource.

> **Isaiah 5:8.** *Woe unto them that join house to house, that lay field to field, till there be no place, that they may be placed alone in the midst of the earth!*

The declaration of "woe" was common among the prophets as they prophesied the imminent destruction of the nations of Israel and Judah. The word refers to the acceptance of a coming destruction. The word was also used by the nation when they realized the potential of their imminent destruction by an enemy,[11] by individuals who recognized their inability to

---

[11] Numbers 21:29;

overcome oncoming destruction.[12] Isaiah is referring to those who have set themselves above others as they are engaged in all manner of intrigue over the covetous acquisition of land.

Though their teaching holds that individuals are only stewards of land that belongs to God, the inheritance of the land because a badge of ownership and position. Those who did not own land were despised. It is this prejudice that is evident in the conflicts between Isaac and Ishmael, Jacob and Esau. By rejecting others, the landed Jews created enemies among all others, not only including their neighboring countries, but among their own families and communities. Samuel's indictment against the Jewish aristocracy may be understood to also state that their penchant for being alone in life will be also granted in death as they will be buried alone in the "midst of the earth," denying them the blessing of "Abraham's Bosom," a traditional place of death for the faithful who awaited the coming of the Messiah. Isaiah identifies that their rejection of God will win for them only an eternity separated from Him and from the remnant of the faithful who will reside in "Abraham's Bosom."

> **Isaiah 5:9-10.** *In mine ears said the LORD of hosts, Of a truth many houses shall be desolate, even great and fair, without inhabitant. ¹⁰Yea, ten acres of vineyard shall yield one bath, and the seed of an homer shall yield an ephah.*

Samuel states that literally, the LORD is in his own ears as He reveals the destruction of the apostate Israel. As the landed Jews have vied over land, their demise will result in its intrinsic worthlessness. As they invested great effort and money into

---

[12] Job 10:15; Psalm 120:5; Proverbs 23:29, e.g.

the accumulation and maintenance of the land, it will return nothing for them. They will be taken from the land, leaving their houses and lands empty. Their crops will lay to waste, whereas ten acres of a vineyard which should produce enough wine to make its owner rich will produce only enough to fill a small container, indicating a devastating financial loss. The idea is simply that all of the investment and priority that they put into the land will result in no gain.

> **Isaiah 5:11-17.** *Woe unto them that rise up early in the morning, that they may follow strong drink; that continue until night, till wine inflame them! [12]And the harp, and the viol, the tabret, and pipe, and wine, are in their feasts: but they regard not the work of the LORD, neither consider the operation of his hands.*

Isaiah repeats the woe that is a curse among those who have disregarded the LORD in their lifestyle. Note that Isaiah is pointing out the "lifestyle of the rich and famous," those who think of themselves as better than others, and those who are considered great by those of little means. Yet, when we look at the true lifestyle of these "great" people, we find idolators who are caught up in their own self-gratifying addictions, blinded by them so that they do not see or appreciate the LORD or His work.

We may, like so many others in history, give great respect and honor to those who have great wealth and power, not realizing that true greatness is not found in that wealth and power. True greatness is found in the humble heart, found only in one who has given all to the LORD. We get caught up in one of satan's lies when we give veneration to the wicked and we despise the lowly. Through Isaiah the LORD clearly defines the state of the wicked rich: a state of woe.

> **Isaiah 5:13.** *Therefore my people are gone into captivity, because they have no knowledge: and their honourable men are famished, and their multitude dried up with thirst.*

With the hand of the LORD's protection, the nation of Israel (and later Judah) will, indeed be destroyed, and its people of note will be taken into captivity. Their land will be taken by the invading king, and distributed to strangers. Where they thought that their lives would continue in their current state of greed and gluttony, they will find only famine and thirst.

At first glance, we may think that this is an unfair judgment of God, but when we consider the nature of God's promise, it is the only possible outcome to Israel's apostasy. God promised to give the "chosen people" the land and keep them safe in it as long as they would be faithful to Him. There were a lot of "If you will…" statements in the covenant between God and man. By rejecting God, Israel walked away from Him, walking away from His protection and giving that task to their surrounding allies who turned against them.

> **Isaiah 5:14.** *Therefore hell hath enlarged herself, and opened her mouth without measure: and their glory, and their multitude, and their pomp, and he that rejoiceth, shall descend into it.*

Isaiah does not hold back the nature of the judgment that is coming upon those in his nation that are leading it into destruction. The "midst of the earth" that he refers to in verse 8 is large enough to contain the souls of those who have turned their back on God and sown a harvest of sin. Isaiah speaks of the greatness, the pomp, and the self-rejoicing that so characterizes those who have been condemned. Their pomp will descend into the depths of sheol along with them.

Isaiah reveals a dramatic judgment against Israel, a nation that has been called by God to be His people, called to obedience to Him. If any people could know the glory and majesty of God, it would have been the nation of Israel, yet even with this knowledge, the replaced their faith in God with a greater faith in the things of this world.

How does this relate to the church today? We may be encouraged to know that Israel was writing to a nation of unfaithful, lost people. They were a group who was unsaved and unregenerate, lacking the resource of the Holy Spirit to lead their hearts to the truth. Consequently, these verses would be inappropriately applied if they are used to communicate a message of condemnation to today's faithful Christians. However, Isaiah's prophecy does clearly identify the consequence of apostasy. As the modern church has, like ancient Israel, moved further and further away from the truth, it is becoming easier for an individual to be part of what they believe to be a Christian fellowship, but remain in their lost state because of that fellowship's low standards of faith.

We saw a great deal of self-importance among the ancient Israelites, and we see that same behavior today among those who claim the faith. We see a great deal of pomp and pride, among the leaders of the larger church fellowships, or among the multi-million-dollar ministries.

God described the work that He has put into the vineyard, work intended to bring a great harvest of good fruit. The early

Israelites were judged by their lack of fruit. Is the church producing a bounty of spiritual fruit today? As a believer, what kind of spiritual fruit are you producing? Is your fruit one that the LORD of the vineyard would cut down and carry to the waste pile, or is it the choice fruit of obedience that produces a bounty of love and grace in the community around you?

Isaiah gives us much to think and to pray about. Let it be a declaration to us to set behind us any encumbrance that would impede us as we strive to press toward the mark of the high calling of God.

Isaiah 6:1-8.
Here Am I, LORD, Send Me!

"Why is there air?" Yes, I am aging myself when I recall this question that was raised by the comedian, Bill Cosby, in the late 1960s. This was back in those days when we would purchase his comedy routines on 33-1/3 RPM LP records.[13] His conclusion as he completed his routine of funny anecdotes is that the purpose for air was to blow up basketballs. When I first heard his comedy routine on the subject as a late teenager, I found myself meditating on the real answer to this question. Why is there air? Without air, we would not exist. God has provided for us an environment that sustains life, and given us a body with a physical set of properties and characteristics that is in equilibrium with it. The elegance and complexity of both is beyond miraculous. By providing this symbiotic environment, God has given us life. Consequently, the real question is a far larger one: Why did God give me life? Why did God give you life? For what purpose has God allowed you and I to take up the space we do and expend the resources of His creation that we do?

When we observe the people of this world we see a very wide spectrum of opinion to the answers to these questions. For most, these questions are probably never considered, as we take for granted our own existence and the state of the universe that we observe. When we do this, there is no need for us to include God in our lives. We simply eke out our daily routine, trying to find some point and direction to it all as we wander in our pursuit of the true abundance of peace and joy that we have been promised by God[14] but not attainable without Him. Paul reminds us that God has revealed himself to all people,[15] and as we become familiar with God's progressive revelation of Himself to mankind through Biblical history, we are encouraged to find that there is a plan and purpose to it all, a plan laid down by God[16] for the benefit of those who serve Him, for those who respond to His call into relationship with Himself.

At the time that Isaiah prophesied to Israel and Judah, the two divided kingdoms were engaged in extreme turmoil. The kingdoms had lost the original understanding of the covenant that God made with them at Mt. Sinai, replacing the characteristics of Godly life that God had given them through the teachings of Moses, and replaced then with a legalistic system of laws that regulated those teachings. The focus shifted from serving a personal God, to serving the impersonal Law. God was no longer needed as they had, over about a 700 year period, wandered from the practice of faith to the practice of religion. The nations wandered aimlessly as they were battered to-and-fro by the political and social tides they immersed themselves in. By rejecting the covenant that they made with God at Mt. Sinai, they chose to leave behind them the hand of His protection, abdicating their end of a promise that would have kept them in the land under God's hand of protection. The northern kingdom of Israel would be utterly destroyed within 20 years of Isaiah's first prophecy. The

---

[13] Bill Cosby, *Why is there Air?* August 1978, Recorded at the Flamingo Hotel, Las Vegas, NV. Allen Sherman, Roy Silver procucers.
[14] John 10:10.
[15] Romans 1.

people would lose the land and their identity as they were taken captive in Assyria and the land was repopulated with peoples from other lands. The Northern culture of Jewish Israel was never heard from again. The southern Kingdom of Judah would suffer the same fate, though God's protection of the faithful remnant that remained in the Southern kingdom did result in their keeping the land for a longer period. It was not until the influence of the faithful was completely absent from the leadership was the southern nation destroyed by Babylon. God still honored his promise to protect the remnant of faithful when they were taken to Babylon, and He honored his promise to give them the land when they returned to it under the leadership of Ezra and Nehemiah about 70 years after the initial captivity. However, with only Judah and part of the tribe of Benjamin represented by the returning remnant, the land they occupied under God's hand was only that of Judah.

So, as Isaiah looks around himself, he sees a nation of Jews who have wandered away from their commitment to God and is aware of the consequences of their apostasy. Brought up close to the government and close to the temple, he was in a position and place where God could use Him. Because of his faith in God, he was also available to be used by God. In many ways, the placement of Isaiah in this apostate nation is not unlike the placement of faithful Christians in this apostate world today.

> **Isaiah 6:1.** *In the year that king Uzziah died I saw also the Lord sitting upon a throne, high and lifted up, and his train filled the temple.*

With the lack of a formal annual calendar, the ancient Jews recorded their events in relation to the coronation of their kings.

---

[16] Romans 8:28.

Uzziah died somewhere within 747 to 735 B.C. As Paul has written, God has revealed Himself to mankind in many ways. However, God chose to grant the faithful Isaiah a unique and special gift, one that would embolden his faith for the remainder of his days: God gave sight to Isaiah's faith. We exhibit faith when we stand firmly on that which we have not seen. We trust in the truth of the Word of God, and we do see God's handiwork all around us. However, there are very few who have actually had the opportunity to get a glimpse of what the true and full nature of God and heaven is like. Those who have had such an experience are among a few, yet these few have each had a dramatic impact on the world as they served God without reservation after meeting Him in such a personal way. Jesus said, "Blessed are those who have not seen and yet believed."[17] This is where you and I are. God will probably not grant to us the depth of vision and understanding that He granted Isaiah, so we must respond on faith rather than on sight.

What did Isaiah see? Of course, Isaiah's first reference is to the appearance of the Lord, Yahweh. "Sitting on the throne" is a clear reference to authority. Worldly kings traditionally sat on thrones, and nations placed the one in authority over them on a throne. When a king would be given the throne, he would be given the authority to rule the kingdom. This is imagery that the ancient Jew can clearly understand. They lived in a time and culture when kingdoms rose and fell as nations vied against nations. Each spring was the time for the kings to go off to war[18] to expand the area of their authority. At such a time of intense intrigue, Isaiah points out where the true authority is. The authority is not held by King Uzziah, who though a somewhat godly king, never removed the pagan worship from the kingdom. The true authority is not in the

---

[17] John 20:29.
[18] 2 Samuel 11:1.

kings of the neighboring tribes and nations. The people can be encouraged to know that with all of the seemly chaotic events that we bring upon ourselves, God is still the one supreme authority.

Isaiah also points out that the throne is elevated to an extreme height. Again when we look at ancient culture, the high ground was always considered that place of the greatest security and power. The tops of mountains were considered holy places in nearly every ancient near-eastern culture. When we combine these cultural understandings, we see that God's authority is the One authority that is immediate and preeminent, standing high above all others. God stands on an authority that will never be overrun, as a opposed to the imminent destruction the thrones of Israel and Judah.

The "train" of a king referred to that which follow Him closely. We think of a train as an extension of a robe, still common today on women's wedding gowns. When a bride ascends the altar, she will often have bridesmaids who serve her by managing her train. This is not dissimilar imagery to what Isaiah is describing. He sees the authority of God, fully sovereign, and He is not alone. God is surrounded by the faithful, those who honor and worship Him.

This is the image that God had planned for mankind. The covenant He made with Abraham, and with his seed through Moses, was a covenant that if unbroken would have been characterized by the image that Isaiah sees. The encouragement to us and to the ancients is that God is on the throne, there is a blessed remnant of the faithful who will always remain, and his plan will be fully accomplished.

Isaiah 6:2. *Above it stood the seraphims: each one had six wings; with twain he covered his face, and with twain he covered his feet, and with twain he did fly.*

When we look at the huge diversity of the flora and fauna of this world, should we be any less surprised to learn of a variety of creatures in heaven? Whether the creatures that Isaiah describes are literal or symbolic is uncertain, particularly when it is sometimes difficult to ascertain whether we are reading apocalyptic literature which presents concrete theological truths using an intense form of imagery. The only biblical reference to the seraphim is in the sixth chapter of Isaiah.[19] However, we find the cherubim of Revelation 4:8 similar to the seraphim, and they could be representing the same beings. There is no doubt that Isaiah describes the seraphim as living creatures who demonstrated true reverence and worship in the presence of God.

The seraphim are described has having three pairs of wings, each serving a purpose. The intended purpose of wings is to provide the power to take flight. Certainly, the Seraphim would fly best if all six wings were used for this purpose. However, with one set of wings the seraphim covered their faces, a clear reference to their recognition of the infinity of God's honor, an honor that is so "high and lifted up" that they do not deserve to look upon Him. This represents their understanding of the glory of God.

The second set of wings was used to cover their feet. To the ancient near-eastern cultures, the covering of one's feet was an idiomatic expression of humility. As the seraphim recognized the glory of God, they also recognized their own

---

[19] Note the "im" on the end of the name is plural, so placing an "s" on the end is redundant.

place in God's presence and did not come to God in a prideful manner, but in one of abject humility.

Finally, with the third set of wings, they flew. Fully recognizing the glory of God, and fully understanding their own place of humility in His presence, the seraphim were able to fulfill their purpose.

Again, the appearance of the seraphim is similar to the image that God planned for mankind. If we truly respond to God as He has planned and allowed, we will recognize His unfathomable Glory and our own humility. It is not until we have reached that point can we truly and fully respond to Him as He desires. When we fully respond to God in the manner of the seraphim, we can fully accomplish the purpose that God has for us.

There is a lesson here that may be profitable for us if we recognize what the seraphim are doing with their wings, and why they are doing it. They are giving up some of their power to fly in order to fly within God's will and purpose for them. When we fully understand the majesty and glory of God we would also be tempered in our response to Him, recognizing that He is too holy to be looked upon and we are too lowly to be in His presence.

> **Isaiah 6:3.** *And one cried unto another, and said, Holy, holy, holy, is the LORD of hosts: the whole earth is full of his glory.*

The response to the seraphim in worship is clear. They repeat the *trisagion*, the "Holy, holy, holy" that is repeated here and in Revelation 4:8 by various heavenly creatures who also are described with six similarly applied sets of wings.

What Isaiah is witnessing is the nature of true worship. As a faithful servant of God, how frustrated must Isaiah be by what he sees as the powerless form of worship inside and outside the Jerusalem temple when he has had such an opportunity to know the characteristics of true worship? Christians come together to worship God, usually at quite well planned weekly meetings where we go through an "order of worship" that will follow the traditions of our denominational lines. The worship service starts and stops on time. If it does not stop on time, many in attendance will become annoyed. Is this worship? Somewhere, the worship of God as described by Isaiah has been replaced with an event that is designed for our own entertainment. We want to hear the songs we like. We want to hear the positive and heart-warming messages that make us feel good. We applaud the inspirational music presentations while responding quietly to those that are not quite so dramatic. Where is the worship? This is what Isaiah is asking when he enters the Jerusalem temple.

Again, the worship that Isaiah describes is the worship that God has planned for mankind all along. It is a spontaneous display of praise and adoration, presented by those who fully recognize God's infinite glory, their own humility, and God's plan and purpose for their lives.

> **Isaiah 6:4.** *And the posts of the door moved at the voice of him that cried, and the house was filled with smoke.*

God has on other occasions revealed Himself physically to mankind through tremors[20] and a cloud of smoke.[21] God is far more than a simple authority on a throne. As the Creator and Lord, He interacts with his creation in a powerful and dynamic

---

[20] Exodus 19:18, Acts 4:31.
[21] Exodus 33:9 et. al.

way. Some always argue that "there is no God" as they wander through their pointless existence. They do not see the work of God in their own lives or in the world[22] around them. As our faith increases we begin to see God more and more as we come to recognize more clearly His work around us. How wonderful would it be to be able to visually gaze upon the Glory of God? If that glory were visible to man today, what would happen? Something similar happened with the pillar of fire that stood over the tent of meeting in the wilderness and over the temple for the 800 years from the Exodus to the Exile. The people's awe lasted only a few days, and the pillar of fire was largely ignored for the remaining years. Only Ezekiel speaks of the removal of the Glory of God from the temple after Judah was taken by Babylon.

It would be wonderful to see that pillar of fire, but we know that God's plan is one of faith, not one of sight as He calls us to Him through the desire of our heart rather than through some showy miracle. Even today, a pillar of fire would be front page news only for a few days, and then later relegated to the religion page, and then it would become a paid tourist attraction. Its presence would soon be explained away by scientists, so even with the appearance of the pillar, faith would still be necessary.

We are reminded by Isaiah of the indescribable power and glory of God, that He is worthy to be properly worshipped, and we have the opportunity to do so.

> **Isaiah 6:5.** *Then said I, Woe is me! for I am undone; because I am a man of unclean lips, and I dwell in the midst of a people of unclean lips: for mine eyes have seen the King, the LORD of hosts.*

---

[22] Isaiah 6:9-10.

When this setting is considered from Isaiah's point of view he is presented with a significant problem. Their tradition held that no person could look upon the face of God and live.[23] The sin that we harbor in our hearts (**unclean lips**) separates us from the One Holy God. However, when we look at the humility experienced by those who did see God,[24] we find that they did not physically die as a response to the event. Certainly, their lives were dramatically changed: each died to their old way of life. <u>To see the face of God is not to die physically, but to die to the old sin-nature when one turns to God</u>. Isaiah is about to learn this wonderful lesson. We cannot stand before a Holy God while stained by our sinfulness, and we have no means by which to find atonement for that sin. Only God can forgive us of our sin as an act of His grace, given to those whom He loves. It is only when we see His face and die to that sin are we truly saved.

> **Isaiah 6:6-7.** *Then flew one of the seraphims unto me, having a live coal in his hand, which he had taken with the tongs from off the altar: ⁷And he laid it upon my mouth, and said, Lo, this hath touched thy lips; and thine iniquity is taken away, and thy sin purged.*

Again, we cannot come before the Lord while standing guilty in our sin. The image that Isaiah demonstrates to us involves both fire and pain. Somehow, because of our natural penchant for wanting a rewards-punishment system, we are never satisfied that we have paid a debt unless some modicum of pain is experienced. Though grace is painless, our willingness to receive it may not be. Isaiah used the metaphor of his lips to

---

[23] Gen. 32:30, Jud. 6:22-23, et. al.
[24] i.e. Isaiah, Jacob, Gideon, John.

represent the sins in his own life and those of all people, and for many of us the lips may be a quite reasonable focal point.

> **Matthew 15:16b-20.** *Jesus said, Are ye also yet without understanding? ^{17}Do not ye yet understand, that whatsoever entereth in at the mouth goeth into the belly, and is cast out into the draught? ^{18}But those things which proceed out of the mouth come forth from the heart; and they defile the man. ^{19}For out of the heart proceed evil thoughts, murders, adulteries, fornications, thefts, false witness, blasphemies: ^{20}These are the things which defile a man: but to eat with unwashen hands defileth not a man.*

Note that the forgiveness of sin required no act on Isaiah's part other than to humbly submit to God. Isaiah did not have to do any great work, or pay any great debt. He did not have to suffer some great penalty to pay for his sins. There is no act of atonement that we can use to earn God's forgiveness. Forgiveness is simply a free gift, a gift that only God can give. Still the penalty for sin must be paid. We find that whether we use biblical history after the event of Jesus' crucifixion, or the prophesies that were presented before, that it was the act of submission to death by Jesus, the Messiah and creator at the cross of Calvary that paid the sin debt for all who place their faith and trust in God, whether they lived prior to the Crucifixion or afterward. Isaiah was receiving the benefit of Jesus' crucifixion as God forgave him and took away his iniquity.

This same offer of forgiveness is given to all who will place their faith and trust in God.

Isaiah 6:8. *Also I heard the voice of the Lord, saying, Whom shall I send, and who will go for us? Then said I, Here am I; send me.*

In one of the most well-known statements in the book of Isaiah, we see an illustration of how we will respond to God when we come to fully embrace His glory, our humility, and His purpose: we respond in obedience to His call. We cannot come to fully know God and simply turn our backs and walk away. Many have heard of God and learned of the opportunity of grace that he offers, yet they still reject Him.[25] Isaiah came to a point in his life where his faith in God was full and complete. It is at this point that God can begin to apply His purpose for Isaiah's life. We have an image of a faithful follower of God who is then presented by God with a real purpose and direction: "Who shall I send, and who will go for us."

God has called every Christian to ministry. We see in Jesus' last address to the disciples that we are to "*Go, and make disciples.*"[26] We might observe some of the nature of Isaiah's response to God's call and see how this applies to our own lives.

- Isaiah did not spend four years in college and another three to five in a theological seminary before God could use him. Isaiah was simply a man who loved God. Loving God is the only preparation that is needed to begin serving Him.

- Isaiah did not know what the task would be. God did not reveal where Isaiah would go, or what He would be called to do. In Isaiah's faithfulness, he simply exhibited a willingness to follow God's call

---
[25] Hebrews 6:4, ff.

without regard to where it would take him or to what task he would accomplish.

We can easily get ourselves tied down in our little world of entangling responsibilities and relationships. As we look for God's place of service for us, we often want to stay in our own comfortable back yard. We have established a comfort zone with boundaries that we protect at all costs. Are you willing to simply pull up your "roots" that you have so firmly planted for yourself and go to a different place where God wants you to serve Him? You may be part of a fellowship of talented and faithful Christians who enjoy one another's company and give a lot of thought to those around the world who are without a witness of God's love, and are obedient to learn about and pray for the needs for those outside the comfort zone of the church, yet few actually follow God's call into the field. Our churches become fortresses of religion and practice while those outside of the walls are despised by the church and left to die without ever knowing the Lord. We do not have to travel across the world to find the mission field. For most of us, we need only look out our bedroom window.

What we see in Isaiah is a willingness that is so sincere, that it is combined with a firm commitment. God showed Isaiah that it is His purpose that people of faith would submit to His call to spread the good news of His Word throughout the world. Isaiah's response to hearing of the need of kingdom work is simple, "*Here am I, send me.*" One can see Isaiah's response like that of a trusting child who eagerly raises his waving hand in the schoolroom when the teacher calls for a volunteer. Imagine the boldness of such a statement, shouted out in the presence of God and His train, a statement that was not directed specifically at him. So many of us sit and wait for God's call to be spoken into our ears. We will not move until

---

[26] Matthew 28:18 ff.

we have heard the clear voice of God call us by name, individually, to a specified task. God reveals the need for kingdom work all around us, all the time. He has revealed it in His word, and He is speaking it now to your own heart. Isaiah heard of the need and simply responded, "Send me!"

Obedience is not characterized by waiting for a miraculous word of God.

Obedience is characterized by acting upon a willingness to serve God when there is kingdom work to be done.

We can see some truths in the call of Isaiah that we probably pay little attention to in our daily lives, and some questions may be raised:

1. **Have we truly appreciated the glory of God?** We fail to really appropriate for ourselves an appreciation for God's glory. We live like God is our "co-pilot" while we are in charge of our world, if we give Him authority at all. We do not see God as Isaiah sees Him, for if we did, our response to Him would be profoundly different.

2. **Is pride standing in our way?** Failing to recognize God's glory, we also live lives that are characterized by pride and self-sufficiency. We see no need for God to intervene in our lives unless our circumstances get desperate. It is at those times that we suddenly want a healing touch from God. It is at those times that we want to receive something from God when we have given Him little or nothing of our own lives.

3. **Why do we not truly worship?** Failing to embrace God's glory and our own humble state, we fail to truly worship God. We go through motions, religions practices, rites, sing songs,

listen to or recite prayers. We may do many "things" that may help us to focus on God, but do we really and truly worship Him?

4. **Why are we so hesitant to serve?** God has revealed Himself, His plan, and the need for the spread of the gospel. This is not rocket science. Yet we wait, and we wait, and we wait ... What are we waiting for? Our testimony is "God, send someone else"

I have never forgotten a song written by Scott Wesley Brown and Phill McHugh, though my memory of the lyrics may not be exact:

> *Oh Lord I am your willing servant*
> *You know that I have been for years*
> *I'm here in this pew every Sunday and Wednesday*
> *I've stained it with many a tear*
> *I've given You years of my service*
> *I've always given my best*
> *And I've never asked you for anything much*
> *So, Lord I deserve this request:*
>
> *Please don't send me to Africa ...*[27]

This is just the first part of a tragic song that illustrates the state of many Christians today who sit in their pews and fail to serve. Their pews become the venue from which to exercise criticism as they seek to be entertained with a worship experience that is shaped to their own liking, only to leave and live among the peoples of the world without being touched.

---

[27] Scott Wesley Brown, Phill McHugh. Please Don't Send Me to Africa. Copyright 1988 Universal Music - Brentwood Benson Publishing Pamela Kay Music River Oaks Music. Administered by Brentwood-Benson Music Publishing, Inc., Capitol CMG Publishing.

Let each of us look into our own hearts and take inventory of where we stand in our commitment to God. If we have never given our heart and life to God, then we stand before him in our iniquity, with our sin unforgiven. The wages of sin is eternal separation from Him,[28] so our only choice for salvation is simple: trust God.

If we have put our trust in God, it is His plan for that relationship we have with him to develop so that we can know the peace and joy that He offers, and be a part of His plan to bring His love to a lost world. It is God's plan that the good news of His grace be communicated clearly to those who need to hear by those who know the truth. God's plan for the salvation of all mankind involves the witness of every believer. We need not wait for a letter: it is in His word. We need not wait on His voice: it is in His word. All we need do is stand next to Isaiah and with him declare in a shout, "Lord, send me!"

---

[28] Romans 3:23.

Isaiah 7:1-16.
Trust the Good News of God

Times of stress can serve to expose much of the truth of who we really are. When times are going well and we are free from difficulties, it can be easy to become self-dependent and minimize the extent or impact of many of the dangers or pitfalls that truly do threaten us. People often focus less and less on the truth of their spiritual needs when their physical needs are fully met. Many people of faith maintain a very weak to almost non-existent relationship with their own fellowship of faith for extended numbers of years until some major event enters their lives and they find themselves in need. It is only until then that they remember their need for the LORD and seek out the church and its membership for assistance.

Self-sufficiency and self-satisfaction can be on of the most subtle of dangers in the life of an individual, particularly when they promote an independence from God. To ignore God and assume that all of one's blessings are a natural part of this world and obtained only by one's own hands is ignorant and dangerous. It is ignorant simply because every good blessing in this universe is there only because of the Grace of God who created it all.[29] Second, by refusing to acknowledge the working of God in one's life, one has separated one's self from Him, and if this leads to a lifetime without a profession of

---

[29] Jasmes 1:17.

sincere faith in God, the justified end is an eternity apart from the Holy Spirit, a profoundly dangerous possibility.

When this self-sufficiency is passed from generation to generation there is the likelihood that little of the faith of the parents is passed on to the children, and soon the knowledge and understanding of God is severely reduced. This is what happened to those who followed after Abraham. Though Abraham passed his faith on to Isaac, who passed it on to Jacob, and he to his twelve sons, it did not take long for this pattern to break down. The twelve sons raised their families in northern Egypt, and many generations later were delivered from Egypt by God through Moses and returned to the land of Canaan. The faith of their fathers was all but lost, remaining only in a non-influential remnant of what now was a divided nation of Israel and Judah. By placing their trust in alliances with warring nations, the Jews found themselves a pawn of their wars. What they had understood as self-sufficiency and self-satisfaction is about to prove to be the undoing of the nation.

> **Isaiah 7:1.** *And it came to pass in the days of Ahaz the son of Jotham, the son of Uzziah, king of Judah, that Rezin the king of Syria, and Pekah the son of Remaliah, king of Israel, went up toward Jerusalem to war against it, but could not prevail against it.*

The time of this setting is determined by the confluence of the reign of three kings. Ahaz became the king of Judah in 735 B.C. succeeding his belated father, Jotham, son of Uzziah. We may recall from Isaiah 6:1 that it was in the year of Uzziah's death that God called Isaiah. The other two kings mentioned are Pekah the king of the northern nation of Israel and Rezin, the king of Syria. The people of Syria, referred to also as Arameans, were from the tribe of Aram, grandson of Noah.[30]

Another player in the current setting of political intrigue is Tiglath-Pileser III,[31] the king of Assyria[32] who is, at this time, expanding his kingdom, taking authority over Judah, Syria, and Israel, exacting tribute from them. Faced with a common enemy, Pekah King of Israel allied with Rezin, king of Syria. Included in the alliance were the Philistines and other small nations. However, Ahaz, king of Judah refused to form an alliance with the pagan nations. Shared enemies produce alliances among these nomadic kings, and the refusal of Judah's Ahaz to join the alliance marked him as an enemy of Israel. Consequently, with Judah perceived as an enemy, Pekah and Rezin in an unholy alliance, made plans to remove Ahaz from the throne of Judah and replace him with a puppet of their own. The passage reveals that they started a military action against Judah, and history reveals their capture of the smaller cities. However, they were not able to prevail against Ahaz.

What is wrong here? Did Israel forget that Judah is a blood-brother nation? In this alliance we find that Israel was depending entirely on its own power and the power of its alliances to protect itself against the more powerful king Tiglath-Pilezer III. Israel had a far more powerful ally to draw from during this period of intrigue: God, the LORD of their salvation. As the king of Israel, Pekah should have been leading the nation to faith in God, not faith in his own alliances with pagan neighbors.

---

[30] Genesis 10:22.
[31] Also referred to as "Pul," 2 Kings 19:15.
[32] Reigned from 744-727 B.C.

Isaiah 7:2. *And it was told the house of David, saying, Syria is confederate with Ephraim. And his heart was moved, and the heart of his people, as the trees of the wood are moved with the wind.*

Ahaz found himself in an untenable situation. With no allies he faced what looked like inevitable defeat. How many times do we, in our own lives, face similar, if not quite as dramatic, situations? When we leave the protection of the LORD and strike out on our own, we can accomplish nothing greater than ourselves, and we give up the One ally who can deliver us from any situation He chooses, whether it be physical, spiritual, emotional, relational, etc. Like the intrigue of Israel, the intrigue we bring into our own lives can be equally destructive. As we look a the world today we see the remnant of the faithful shrinking in what the rest of the world thinks is a world that does not need God. Families are being destroyed in record numbers, and much of what has been considered foundational to civilization is crumbling.

When Ahaz heard that Israel had joined with Syria in the battle for Jerusalem, he and the people were "trembling and shaking like the leaves of a tree in the wind."[33] Just as Ahaz is finding himself alone against a world of enemies, the faithful remnant to day finds itself under increasing attack. Those who stand against Christianity are joining ranks. Journal articles and political positions are in agreement as they testify to the decreasing population and influence of Christianity in society today. This decreases is much like it was in ancient Israel as those of faith were replaced with those without faith, and ultimately, the diminishing remnant that remained in Judah was all alone.

---

[33] Isaiah 7:2, paraphrase.

> **Isaiah 7:3.** *Then said the LORD unto Isaiah, Go forth now to meet Ahaz, thou, and Shearjashub thy son, at the end of the conduit of the upper pool in the highway of the fuller's field;*

It is easy to become discouraged when one feels persecuted and alone. Ahaz and the Judeans had few places to find encouragement. However, God's purpose would not be thwarted, and God's promise to preserve the remnant is sure. The reference to the House of David in verse 2 is a reminder of that promise.[34] That promise is also mentioned in the name of Isaiah's son, Shearjashub, meaning "a remnant will return."

Preparing for an impending siege, Ahaz was visiting the city water supply, presumably to insure its integrity. It would be here, at Ahaz' point of preparation that the LORD would send Isaiah with a message of needed encouragement.

> **Isaiah 7:4-5.** *And say unto him, Take heed, and be quiet; fear not, neither be fainthearted for the two tails of these smoking firebrands, for the fierce anger of Rezin with Syria, and of the son of Remaliah. ⁵Because Syria, Ephraim, and the son of Remaliah, have taken evil counsel against thee, saying, 6Let us go up against Judah, and vex it, and let us make a breach therein for us, and set a king in the midst of it, even the son of Tabeal:*

Isaiah brings to Ahaz a message that was probably quite unexpected. Facing these two aligned and warring nations

---

[34] 2 Samuel 7.

without an ally, Ahaz is preparing for his destruction at their hands. His removal from the throne by these enemies means certain death for him. However Isaiah gives the king several words of advice that come from the LORD's revelation to Isaiah of Judah's true situation.

Take heed. First, Isaiah calls upon Ahaz to listen to the word of the LORD. Ahaz is caught up in the circumstances of political intrigue, and is not giving attention to the LORD, nor of His provision for Judah. Ahaz is paying attention to the wrong voices, and needs to return to listening to the voice of God. Also translated as "be careful," Isaiah's advice implies the care with which Ahaz should be taking in his decisions.

Be quiet. One of the voices that is misleading Ahaz at this time of stress is his own. When we listen to our own voice, the resource of wisdom that we are tapping is no greater than our own. Listening to God's voice necessitates diminishing our own.

Fear not. Ahaz' fears are based upon his assessment of the situation without his having all of the facts. His lack in trusting in God has led him to think the worst is going to happen, and as a king, he is responsible to be prepared for that worst-case scenario. However, his fears are unfounded because God still plans on protecting the faithful remnant.

Be strong. Isaiah advises Ahaz to stand strong against this threat, particularly because the threat is not as significant as it appears. The words rendered "smoking firebrands" is an idiom that refers to a burning ember that has no more flame, but is reduced only to smoke. The implication that the threats of Rezin and Pekah are diminished by their own impending demise. Ahaz need not be concerned about their threats because their power is quickly ebbing.

The contempt that is held for these two threatening kings is illustrated by Isaiah's reference to Pekah as the "Son of Remaliah," rather than even acknowledging his name. Isaiah furthermore illustrates the futility of Rezin and Pekah's plan by noting that it is their intent to terminate the Davidic line of kings by placing a "Son of Tabeal" on the throne. Any attempt to destroy the Davidic line is an attempt to thwart God's promise to Israel, engaging God's hand in the battle. Isaiah is reminding Ahaz that God's purpose is engaged in this battle, and Ahaz has no need for any political ally if he will simply trust in God's hand of protection.

> **Isaiah 7:7.** *Thus saith the Lord GOD, It shall not stand, neither shall it come to pass.*

Having given Ahaz a detailed description of God's purpose in this event, he then brings the word of the LORD directly to the king: this attempt by Pekah and Rezin to remove Ahaz from the throne will never take place. Period. End of discussion. We might note that Isaiah presents the word of the LORD in the form of poetry, suitable for placing to music. This was often done to make it easier to remember the words.

How many times do we find ourselves in fear of events in this life that never take place? Instead of relying on God, we can often find ourselves relying on ourselves and are completely unaware of how God is working in our lives to protect us and bring us closer to Himself. We may lay awake at night fearing a job loss, fueled by our own inappropriate feelings of inadequacy, having no idea that our job is secure because our administration trusts in our integrity, loyalty, and excellent job skills, each being unbeknown fruits of our faith.

A life of faith is not characterized by fear. A life of faith stands confidently upon God's grace and promises, and trusts in Him. We fall into fear when we recognize our own inability to protect ourselves against a threat. That fear ebbs when we recognize that God is big enough to protect us. Had Ahaz recognized God's purpose for Judah and for him as its king, he would have never feared the threats of his pagan neighbors, and instead trusted in God. That same trust would have led him to be a godly king over Judah, further improving the life situation of the nation. However, Ahaz was not a man of faith, and did not lead the nation as God desires.

> **Isaiah 7:7-9.** *For the head of Syria is Damascus, and the head of Damascus is Rezin; and within threescore and five years shall Ephraim be broken, that it be not a people. ⁹And the head of Ephraim is Samaria, and the head of Samaria is Remaliah's son. If ye will not believe, surely ye shall not be established.*

Sometimes we inflate the power of our threats in our own mind. Isaiah advises that, when he looks at the two threatening nations which may appear vast and powerful, that these nations are driven by a single city, and that single city is driven by a single man. The threat to Ahaz is not Syria and Israel,[35] nor is it Damascus and Samaria. The threat is from Pekah and Rezin, two men who lack the power to fulfill their threats against Judah, the true remnant of the faithful.

Isaiah also brings an amazing prophecy, one that fully validates his status as a prophet of the LORD. He states that within sixty-five years the northern nation of Israel will no longer exist as a nation. The prophecy is uncanny, for during these next years would include Tiglath-Pileser III's invasion, the fall of Samaria to Sargon II, and the dissolution of the Israelite population under Esar-Haddon. Resin's Syria would also fall to the Assyrian expansion, yet during this time Judah would still stand.

> **Isaiah 7:10-12.** *Moreover the LORD spake again unto Ahaz, saying, [11]Ask thee a sign of the LORD thy God; ask it either in the depth, or in the height above. [12]But Ahaz said, I will not ask, neither will I tempt the LORD.*

Sometimes it is amazing how God is willing to meet us at our own point of need. This prophecy was hard for Ahaz to believe. Why would he take the word of Isaiah against the profound evidence that he perceives around him? Why would we accept the word of a pastor when we have so much evidence that seems contrary to his encouraging advice? Isaiah knew that it was going to be difficult to convince Ahaz of the truth of his prophecy, and God intervened in a significant way, revealing his offer to Ahaz: test me. It was common for pagans to seek a sign from the gods in order to formulate a significant decision. Signs are an inappropriate vehicle for faith-based decisions since the (1) individual identifies an event as a sign without any real validation, and (2) interprets that perceived sign based upon one's own perspective. Furthermore, (3) we tend to "demand" that God would send a sign before we would make a decision, and by so doing diminishing the glory of God to the position of our servant as we put Him to the test. However, Ahaz was so accustomed to pagan practice that God actually allowed Ahaz to seek a sign.

---

[35] The name of Ephraim and Israel are interchangeable. Ephraim is the largest of the ten tribes of the northern nation.

We often still look for "signs," in the decision making process. This passage should be a reminder for us that such behavior is an inappropriate expression of Christian faith. Guidance is not found in signs, but rather in God's Word and through listening to the Holy Spirit in prayer. We also find God's will as the Holy Spirit leads us to understand and appreciate God's working through circumstances and through the lives of other Christians. None of these require interpretation, they simply require submissive
listening.

We see that Ahaz' understanding of the tenets of faith at least recognized the inappropriateness of seeking a sign. He flatly refused to do so.

> **Isaiah 7:13-16.** *And he said, Hear ye now, O house of David; Is it a small thing for you to weary men, but will ye weary my God also? [14]Therefore the Lord himself shall give you a sign;*

Still, despite Ahaz' refusal to request a sign, the LORD would meet Ahaz at his point of need, and send a sign. Isaiah reminds Ahaz that he is of the House of David, a reference to his protected Davidic line. Furthermore, Isaiah reminds Ahaz of the reliability of a prophecy that comes from one who is close to the LORD. It is one thing to reject the advice of ungodly men, but quite another to reject the advice of the LORD's prophet. Ahaz has voiced his resistance to Isaiah's advice, and clearly opposed him when he refused a sign, a decision that was made based on his understanding of religious tradition rather than upon his listening to the advice of the prophet.

However, Ahaz' desire does not predicate the LORD's purpose of plan. God would send Ahaz a sign anyway, one that would help embolden his faith. However, the LORD would not leave Ahaz to "seek" a sign, nor would He cause Ahaz to "interpret" it, the two errors that are associated with our desire for signs. God would reveal both the identity and the interpretation of the sign.

> **Isaiah 7:14-16.** *Behold, a virgin shall conceive, and bear a son, and shall call his name Immanuel. ¹⁵Butter and honey shall he eat, that he may know to refuse the evil, and choose the good. ¹⁶For before the child shall know to refuse the evil, and choose the good, the land that thou abhorrest shall be forsaken of both her kings.*

This prophecy is given to us as a whole, and can be understood as a whole. It is established within scripture in two separate and valid contexts. The prophecy, within this context, is given to assure Ahaz of the imminence of God's protection and plan for Judah. Subsequent scriptures come back to this prophecy revealing that Isaiah's assurance to Ahaz also points to the coming of the Messiah. This prophecy, therefore, can be appropriately studied and applied within both contexts.

It would be appropriate that we first examine the prophecy within the context of Ahaz's dilemma. The word for "virgin" can be accurately interpreted as both "young woman" and "virgin." This prophecy for Ahaz represents a simple statement of God's deliverance and the length of time within which that deliverance would come. There are still people of faith in Judah, represented by this virgin. Evidence of this faith is shown that within Judah a young woman will bear a son and call his name "Immanuel," which means "God, with us." The young Judean mother understands that God has not left Judah, but is working within the nation to perform His plan and purpose. Furthermore this son will be brought up in the faith. The "butter and honey" refer to the word of God as presented to the people in the scriptures. This young man will be brought up in a family of faith. This is a reminder to Ahaz that Judea is still a nation of faith, the home of the remnant. Finally, before that child is old enough to "choose the good," a reference to the age of accountability, traditionally 12 or 13 years, both Rezin and Pekin will be removed from their respective thrones. Again, an accurate prophecy. Pekah was assassinated ten years later and Tiglath-Pileser III would destroy Rezin and Damascus shortly after Pekin's demise.

Isaiah's prophecy proclaimed the immediate deliverance of Ahaz from his enemies. However, the larger context of this prophecy is well-accepted and understood as it is referenced from later scripture as pointing to the context of the coming Messiah. Within this context we find the amazing understanding that "virgin" would refer to the immaculate conception of Mary, the mother of Jesus. Ahaz would not have understood that interpretation of the word, and it is possible that Isaiah would not have either. Another miracle that fulfills Isaiah's prophecy is the nature of the child, Jesus, who is clearly "God, with us."

The experience of Ahaz and pre-exilic Judah is a reminder of us that God meets us at our point of need as we experience the conflicts of our daily lives. He has ordained the protection of those who serve Him, and has promised an eternal and blessed home with Him through the work of the Messiah, Jesus. This is the good news of the truth.

What happens when we reject the truth of the gospel? Anything but the gospel is simply a lie that we fall into when we listen to the messages of this world. Ahaz was listening to the messages of the world and would not completely accept Isaiah's prophecy. He would later approach Tiglath-Pilezer III for "protection" from Pekin and Rezin, ignoring Isaiah's advice. Ahaz would pay tribute to Pilezer that included emptying the temple treasury,[36] accomplishing in an administrative choice something that Judah's armies had avoided over years of protection, and by so doing changed Judah from an independent nation to a vassal of Assyria. Ahaz sold out to Assyria.

However, God's purpose will not be undone by man's lack of faith. The Messiah would eventually come, God with Us, the Christ, Jesus. We can, like Ahaz, refuse to hear the good news of the gospel and rather than accept His offer of grace, choose to make our allegiance with the world, choosing separation from God. However, God has spoken through scriptures, through Isaiah, and finally through Jesus Christ to communicate to us His eternal deliverance from the destructive powers of this world. We would not be so wise to follow Ahaz. We can follow Jesus.

---

[36] 2 Kings 16:5-20.

Isaiah 17:1-14.
All Are Accountable

The date is between 735 - 732 B.C. The northern nation of Israel has wandered far from its covenant roots that were founded at Mt. Sinai. Rebelling against Rehoboam, king of Judah, grandson of David, the non-Judean tribes broke away and formed this northern kingdom of Israel. The faithful remnant remained in Judah when Israel was formed, leaving the northern kingdom in the hands of ungodly and pagan kings. The holy shrines at Bethel and Dan had become places of pagan worship. The two nations of Judah and Israel had turned from God and chose to govern themselves in the manner of their neighboring countries, anointing kings to rule over themselves. These kings entered into alliances with their warring neighbors, sweeping them into their wars and conflicts. By 730 B.C., Israel chose to consummate an alliance with pagan Damascus in order to avoid being overrun by the giant nation of Assyria, and by doing so chose sides in Assyria's conflicts with Babylon and Ethiopia/Egypt, the other two large militant nations in the region. The southern nation of Judah refused to enter into this alliance against Assyria, prompting Damascus to attack Judah. Israel is standing with Damascus against Judah in what is known as the Syro-Ephraimite war.

Isaiah 17:1. *The burden of Damascus. Behold, Damascus is taken away from being a city, and it shall be a ruinous heap.*

The word translated, "burden" is frequently translated "oracle," and the content of Isaiah's writing is probably best described as a combination of the two. "Oracle" implies a prophecy, and "burden" describes the nature of that prophecy: a deep and dramatic loss. In his writings, Isaiah teaches of the impending destruction of both Israel and Judah that is the direct result of their rejection of their covenant with God: if they would obey and worship Him and Him alone, God would preserve them in the land of promise. However, they have continually turned from God for approximately 700 years, and they have chosen to remove themselves from God's hand of protection, and seek protection in their alliances with pagan nations. With God's hand removed, it is only a matter of time until these tiny and nearly powerless nations are swept up in the conquests of their large neighbors.

However, Isaiah does not limit his prophecy to the children of Israel. Beginning in Chapter 13, Isaiah writes oracles to Babylon, Assyria, Philistia, and Moab. These nations, like Aram and Damascus it's capitol, had made no covenant with God. What is their accountability towards God? When we look at the contrast between Judah and the pagan nations, we may see a social parallel that exists today in the contrast between Christians and those who have rejected God. The accountability of Christians to God as their Lord is moot. What is the accountability towards God of those who reject His offer of grace? Paul writes in his letter to the Romans (1:20) that God has revealed Himself to all people, and there is consequently no excuse for rejecting Him.

Israel has chosen to put its trust in Damascus, rather than in God. Having rejected God, the doom for Damascus is the same as that of Judah and Israel: God's hand of protection is removed from a people who could have turned to Him in faith. As a city, Damascus formed around the time of King Solomon, so by this time Damascus is grown for about 400 years into one of the largest cities in the region. The city is large enough that it is trying to stand up against Assyria on its own strength and that of the neighbors to the west that it can conquer: Israel and Judah. With it's sights set on the conquest of Judah, Isaiah announces the consequence of Damascus' arrogance.[37] A time will be coming when Damascus will be destroyed. Damascus will be nothing more than a heap of ashes.

> **Isaiah 17:2.** *The cities of Aroer are forsaken: they shall be for flocks, which shall lie down, and none shall make them afraid.*

The arrogance of Damascus will bring destruction not only upon itself, but upon the other cities that look upon it for protection. Aroer is mentioned in several Old Testament passages. "Aroer" literally means "ruins," and its plural usage here probably refers to a cluster of cities. Such cities tended to form around larger cities that the smaller use for commerce and protection, like suburban areas today. The downfall of Damascus will be shared by its surrounding cities.

> **Isaiah 17:3.** *The fortress also shall cease from Ephraim, and the kingdom from Damascus, and the remnant of Syria: they shall be as the glory of the children of Israel, saith the LORD of hosts.*

---

[37] C.f. Isaiah 5:7, 25:2.

Israel's choice to form an alliance with the doomed Damascus will be one of its final acts as a nation. Israel had no military fortress, so by allying with Damascus, Israel hoped that this city would protect it against the growing threat of Assyria. When Damascus falls, Israel will fall with it, along with all that is left of Aram, the remnant of Syria. Considering the 400-year history of the northern kingdom of Israel, its fall is quite imminent. Damascus fell to Assyria in 732 B.C., very shortly after this prophecy, and Israel fell to Assyria only 10 years later.

> **Isaiah 17:4-6.** *And in that day it shall come to pass, that the glory of Jacob shall be made thin, and the fatness of his flesh shall wax lean. ⁵And it shall be as when the harvestman gathereth the corn, and reapeth the ears with his arm; and it shall be as he that gathereth ears in the valley of Rephaim. ⁶Yet gleaning grapes shall be left in it, as the shaking of an olive tree, two or three berries in the top of the uppermost bough, four or five in the outmost fruitful branches thereof, saith the LORD God of Israel.*

"In that day" contains a hit of eschatological judgment. The honor that was once attributed to the nation of Israel will be gone. The end of Israel will be much like the content of the field at harvest time. As a nation, Israel grew from a small seed and had the potential to produce a huge bounty. It is estimated that the time from the birth of Jacob's children to the exile is about 1200 years. If a community of 12 married couples (sons of Israel) are subject to a very conservative pattern of human population growth (1.3 surviving children per adult with average mortality rates), the population of Israel would have grown to over 25 million by the time of the exile. However, the estimated population of Israel and Judah at the time of the exile is far less than this, more in the order of 2 million. This illustrates the extent that Israel assimilated into the pagan culture. As Isaiah illustrates Israel's development as that of a growing harvest, it is quite evident that the harvest itself was not particularly bountiful. Furthermore, the gleaning that Isaiah describes is one of harvesting the apostate, those who have rejected the covenant with God. The gleaning of Israel took place in two passes over the field. First, Assyria destroyed Israel in 722 B.C., and then Babylon destroyed Judah in 587 B.C. Isaiah speaks of the remnant of fruit that is left behind, the two or three berries left in the upper bough, four or five in the outermost branches. This is the remnant of faithful that remained in Judah when it was overrun by Babylon, and many of these were protected by king Nebuchadnezzar when he took them into captivity.

> **Isaiah 17:7-8.** *At that day shall a man look to his Maker, and his eyes shall have respect to the Holy One of Israel. [8]And he shall not look to the altars, the work of his hands, neither shall respect that which his fingers have made, either the groves, or the images.*

When Judah was destroyed by Babylon, the response of the Judeans was nothing less than astonishment. They felt that that Jerusalem was invincible because God was in the temple. To defeat Jerusalem was to them (and their enemies) defeat their God. They experienced an ignorant security in their fortress walls that they had made with their own hands. They had no idea that they could ever lose those things that they had built, whether it be the altars to their pagan gods, the icons they made, or even the commodities they had produced. Isaiah states that when Israel falls, there will be those who will turn back to God. There will be some who will restore their honor and respect for the Holy One of Israel, looking back again to

Him for their security instead of looking to the things of this world.

The Jews came to define their righteousness by the things that they did and the things that they made with their own hands. Some thought that they were righteous simply because they were sons of Abraham. Some thought their righteousness came from their attempt at keeping Mosaic law. Some found their righteousness in the worshipping of icons and images to which they gave an authority greater than themselves. This describes today's culture where people think they are good by keeping to some rule of law, some think they are good because they are members of a good family, or members of a good church. Some still put their trust in things made by man, whether it be the worshipping of icons and images, or if their security is simply found in the hoarding of wealth. The only source of righteousness given to man is that found when one places their faith and trust in God, and in Him alone. The 11th chapter of Hebrews clearly describes how even the patriarchs of the Old Testament were justified by their faith, and not by their works. Isaiah describes the time when some of the Jews will realize this. This is a realization that will come to all people when they come before God at the end of their life on this earth. Will they come before God having placed their trust in the things of this earth, or have they placed their trust in God?

> **Isaiah 17:9-11.** *In that day shall his strong cities be as a forsaken bough, and an uppermost branch, which they left because of the children of Israel: and there shall be desolation. [10]Because thou hast forgotten the God of thy salvation, and hast not been mindful of the rock of thy strength, therefore shalt thou plant pleasant plants, and shalt set it with strange slips: [11]In the day shalt thou*

> *make thy plant to grow, and in the morning shalt thou make thy seed to flourish: but the harvest shall be a heap in the day of grief and of desperate sorrow.*

Israel did not have to build the cities when they entered the Canaanite land of promise. They did not have to plant the fields. When they entered, these were already there, and they simply took them over. When the judgment for their apostasy comes, these cities will be desolate. That which God gave them will be taken away. The blessings that they experience in this world, even in their disobedience, will be lost. Why? By rejecting God, they had no reason to acknowledge that these were a blessing from God. They did not look on the cities and see a gift of God, for they were not mindful of God at all. They experienced the blessings from God without acknowledging that they came from Him. Again, this is a model that is consistent with today's world. Across the world people experience the blessings that this earth provides, whether it be the bounty of crops, the accumulation of wealth, the bounty of loving relationships, or anything else that God has provided. Yet across the world very few people truly acknowledge that all of these blessings come from God, and most people fail to place their faith and trust in Him. Like the ancient Israelites, they follow after other gods, gods of man's fabrication as they embrace the myriad of world religions that reject the truth of God's word. For these, the harvest will be a heap of grief and sorrow when they come before the judgment and be found faithless.

> **Isaiah 17:12-14.** *Woe to the multitude of many people, which make a noise like the noise of the seas; and to the rushing of nations, that make a rushing like the rushing of mighty waters!* [13]*The nations shall rush like the*

rushing of many waters: but God shall rebuke them, and they shall flee far off, and shall be chased as the chaff of the mountains before the wind, and like a rolling thing before the whirlwind. ¹⁴And behold at eveningtide trouble; and before the morning he is not. This is the portion of them that spoil us, and the lot of them that rob us.

When we look at the multitudes of this world, we see an overwhelming number of people and cultures that reject God. By revealing Himself to Abraham, Isaac, and Jacob, (as well as Adam, Noah, and many others in the Old Testament), God presented His true self and His message of salvation to man. During the time of ancient Israel, all people fell into two, mutually exclusive, groups: those who trusted in God, and those who did not. Those who trusted in God remained as a remnant of the children of Abraham and any others who embraced their faith. All others embraced other beliefs, whether they be secular or pagan.

God has not changed, His plan of salvation has not changed, and consequently, the state of the nations of peoples has not changed. The world is populated by those who trust in Him and those who do not. Isaiah describes the noise of the unfaithful like the seas, or the rushing of mighty waters, a roar that has no discernable message. What is the judgment for those who have never placed their faith in God? Isaiah describes is at chaff blown away in a wind, never to be seen again, never to be used for any purpose, separated from the fruit forever. This is the judgment upon those who not only reject God, but also those same people who spoil and rob, or persecute, the people of faith.

As Isaiah presents this oracle, we find that (1) the people of Israel are being held accountable for their covenant with God and will find themselves separated from Him because of their apostasy, and (2) the pagan nations are accountable for their rejection of God, and for their persecution of the faithful remnant. Likewise, (1) the church today is accountable for their covenant with God, and those who call themselves Christians but lack true faith in God will find themselves separated from Him because of their apostasy, and (2) today's pagan and secular nations are accountable for their rejection of the One True God, and for their persecution of the faithful remnant, the Christians.

All people are accountable before God for their faith in Him. The only eternal future for those who reject God is eternal separation from Him. The only eternal security is experienced by those who place their faith and trust in God, the One God who has promised to forgive the faithful of their sin and spare them the condemnation of separation from Himself that sin otherwise demands. The covenant that God has made with the faithful today is the same covenant that He made with Israel at Mt. Sinai. It is the same covenant that He made with Abraham, and the same covenant that He made with Noah, and Adam: God rewards faith and trust in Himself with a promise of eternal protection against the condemnation that sin demands: an eternity separated from God. Why would anyone choose to reject God and experience this judgment? We have the history of Israel to show us the consequence of apostasy. We have the destruction of the pagan cities to show us the consequence of summarily rejecting God.

God has given a task to all Christians to spread the good news of the gospel of salvation to all the world so that none would perish, but all could have an opportunity to place their faith and trust in God. This task is the paramount duty of the church, because all people are accountable before God, and will give that account at the final judgment. God desires the salvation of all people. It is time for the church, the body made up of every individual Christian, to take the task seriously.

Isaiah 28:14-22.
Where Do You Place Your Trust?

When we observe today's world culture, whether Christian, religious, and pagan, we find in place a complex network of trust as we seek to distance ourselves from life's dangers and risks. As humans, we find ourselves smaller and weaker than the systems of government that rule us, unable to defend ourselves adequately against the dangers of crime, concerned about the financial stability of our future, threatened by natural disaster, and often living in fear of the consequences of circumstances that surround us every day. In order to maintain our own safety and security, we fabricate a complex network of defenses against the risks that are inherent to our immersion in a sin-sick world and its unpredictable nature.

In the 1920s, many Americans who were concerned about their future financial security sought to place their security in the stock market. The purchasing of stock, fueled by aggressive and misleading public advertising, turned frantic. People were convinced that their investments would bring great gains. Many borrowed money to purchase stocks that became significantly overvalued, often paying prices ten times that of their true asset value. Most companies responded to this infusion of wealth by investing in capital construction that would prove to bring no appreciable productivity. In 1929 the stock market, as it always does, found its true value and investors and the companies they invested in witnessed the most dramatic loss of wealth in the history of the nation. Those who borrowed to purchase stocks included both individuals and corporations, each finding themselves deep in uncollateralized debt. People and corporations declared bankruptcy, further depressing the market. Many investors took their own lives when faced with the desperate circumstances that they themselves had engendered. The result of this single event was the Great Depression of the 1930s.

The southeastern American coastline is often buffeted by hurricanes, and many of these storms are powerful enough to destroy structures that are not strong enough to hold up against the wind, rain, and storm surge tides. A dramatic example of this is the flooding of New Orleans and the Gulf coast by Hurricanes Katrina and Rita in 2005. When Katrina bore down on New Orleans as a category-4 storm, the city's levees were designed to hold up to only a category-3, and the levees failed. Many people suffered or even died when they ignored the reports of what was a category-5 storm shortly before landfall and they chose to ride out the storm trusting in those small and inadequate levees. The strongest part of the storm came ashore near Gulfport, Mississippi where the largest storm surge in history brought a 20-foot wall of water as much as two and three miles inland. Many people died when they decided to ride out the storm in homes that were simply swept off of their foundations by the water and the debris it carried. The destruction from Katrina and Rita covered 90,000 square miles, leaving behind an inestimable number of demolished homes and businesses. People hoped to be able to trust in the government to alleviate their suffering, but the extent of the storm was far beyond any government or agency to even begin to address.

History is filled with events that have brought great human suffering in circumstances where much of that suffering was unnecessary. The stock crash of 1929 came from the foolish greed of people who ignored the instability of stock investments, and acted in a way that promoted that instability. There was sufficient time for people to leave the threatened areas of the Gulf coast when hurricanes Katrina and Rita came ashore, but people chose to place their trust in levees, homes, and buildings that had stood up to smaller storms in the past.

One of these disasters was predicated by the sins of man, the other by the predictable dynamics of world climate. However, in both cases, the suffering and death that were experienced could have been avoided had people not placed their trust in that which cannot provide them protection. How much suffering do we bring upon ourselves when we place ourselves under the protection of that which cannot fully protect us?

As devastating as disasters of this world may appear, how much more personally disastrous will it be when people come before God at the final judgment and hear the words, "depart from me, I never knew you" (Matt. 7:23)? People place their eternal trust in good works, in religion, or in agnostic apathy, and other things of this world that simply cannot save them from the infallible consequence of their unforgiven sin: separation from God.

> *Isaiah 28:14. Wherefore hear the word of the LORD, ye scornful men, that rule this people which is in Jerusalem.*

A third historical event that follows a similar pattern to those above is recorded in the Old Testament, and is instructive. The nation of Israel, "God's chosen people," had long ago turned its back on God whom they had promised to honor and obey in return for His continued protection in the "promised land" of the covenant at Mt. Sinai (Ex. 34). The nation split into two kingdoms with the small remnant of faithful left in the southern kingdom of Judea. Choosing to be a kingdom under the authority of worldly kings rather than continuing to rely on God as their authority, they became subject to the vagaries of ungodly kings who led the nations further away from God as they exercised their pride and ego. This was also a time when the neighboring military powers of Egypt (Cush), Assyria, and Babylon vied with each other for regional dominance. At this point in history the nation of Assyria was the predominant threat in the region, and all other nations were positioning themselves for defense, including Israel and Judah. Rather than rely on God for their protection, promised at the covenant at Mt Sinai, the northern nation of Israel allied with Damascus, an active enemy of the southern nation of Judah. Likewise, rather than turn to God, the southern nation of Judah looked to Egypt for a defensive alliance. In both cases, Israel and Judah sought foreign military alliances to protect itself from Assyria, making baseless pacts with pagan nations that also desired the conquest of the promised land. Faced with three evil nations, Israel and Judah sought to make pacts with the lesser evils in an attempt to ward off the greatest of the three, ignoring God who promised to protect them against them all.

Though a resident of Israel, the prophet Isaiah delivered the word of God to both nations, pointing out their continued error.

> **Isaiah 31:1.** *Woe to them that go down to Egypt for help; and stay on horses, and trust in chariots, because they are many; and in horsemen, because they are very strong; but they look not unto the Holy One of Israel, neither seek the LORD!*

Israel and Judah placed their trust in horses and chariots rather than the LORD who could truly protect them. The word translated "scornful men" is also frequently translated "mockers." which is the most detestable statement of wickedness used in the Hebrew language. It refers specifically to ones who willfully reject the Word of God in their efforts to lead people away from Him and bring them under their own plan or agenda. This description aptly applies to most of the kings of Judah and all of the kings of Israel. Where God had intended the temple of Jerusalem to be a center of worship, it became quite the opposite as people followed their godless kings and worshipped the idols of the pagan society that they chose to immerse themselves in. They exchanged the true worship of God for a worldly and godless form of worship that they themselves desired. The word of God was not as important to them as was the ways of the world. Consequently, they moved from trusting in God to trusting in the things of the world.

> *Isaiah 28:15. Because ye have said, We have made a covenant with death, and with hell are we at agreement; when the overflowing scourge shall pass through, it shall not come unto us: for we have made lies our refuge, and under falsehood have we hid ourselves:*

The kings of Israel and Judah were making "deals with the devil" for protection against the devil himself. It does not take much wisdom to recognize the foolishness of such a choice. Yet, such choices rarely seem foolish to us when our judgment is clouded by our misinterpretation of circumstances; a misinterpretation that is the product of our own pride and our own desires. What rationalizations do we employ when we choose our own solutions to problems rather than rely on God's promises? Probably one of the most disastrous rationalizations that we employ when making a critical choice is, "I have no choice." Often, ignoring God and ignorant of alternatives, we perceive one illusive solution as our only choice and feel constrained to make a decision that in itself places us in jeopardy. Like the illusionist who misdirects our attention, our interpretation of circumstances can misdirect our response. Also, we may ignore the still, quiet voice of the Holy Spirit who reveals the truth of the situation to us. Those who refuse to flee an impending disaster are making such a misdirected choice. Those who seriously consider suicide are also making such a misdirected choice. Also, those who use any number of rationalizations to refuse to honor the LORD in faith are making such a misdirected choice, a choice that will result in devastation far more significant than any storm of this world.

Rationalization has the power to kill. Thousands failed to evacuate New Orleans for lack of busses when safety was only a 30-minute to an hour's walk away. Consequently, people unnecessarily suffered and died in the days following the storm. When we listen to and follow irrational conclusions that are based upon incorrect information, we are responding to untruths; we make "**lies our refuge**," and by so doing place ourselves under their power rather than under the power and protection of God. Facing the "**overwhelming scourge**" of an Assyrian defeat, the Hebrews thought they could stop it with their military alliances. However, these alliances were with nations that had just as much a desire for conquest as did Assyria, and as soon as their compact would serve its use, Damascus would only choose to destroy Israel, and Egypt would choose only to overrun Judah. Actually, neither nation ever had the opportunity to do so.

What voices do we listen to in times of decision making? Often we can fabricate limitless reasons to follow our own desire rather than our God-given wisdom. Or, we like the ancient Israelites, place ourselves under the protection or leadership of godless people who we empower to make decisions for us and lead us away from God's plan for our protection. The people of Judah and Israel placed their trust in evil and godless kings who made decisions based upon godless advice and their own self-serving egos.

Isaiah 28:16. Therefore thus saith the Lord GOD, Behold, I lay in Zion for a foundation a stone, a tried stone, a precious corner stone, a sure foundation: he that believeth shall not make haste.

We may fail to remember that while Isaiah writes, the temple is still standing in Jerusalem, and the Shekinah Glory of God, the Pillar of Fire that consumes the sacrifice on the Day of Atonement, still stands in the center of Jerusalem, referred to here as Zion. Isaiah uses the symbol of a cornerstone as a metaphor for the sure foundation that the presence of God represents in the lives of the Hebrews as well as for us. Part of the preparation work in the building of a fine stone structure was the setting of the cornerstone, the first and most important stone in the foundation. Unlike other stones in the foundation, this stone was first cut and polished so that its sides were ground perfectly square (**a tried stone**), and when set, it was assured that it was laid level and square with the desired direction of the building walls. If the cornerstone is cut or set incorrectly, it will affect the entire structure since every future measurement is taken from this single stone. That which is set in line with the cornerstone will be true and square. As a metaphor, one can see how the cornerstone stands as the foundation of truth.

God is the cornerstone of all that is life, and the foundation for both Hebrew and Christian faith and doctrine. While the ancient Hebrews were looking everywhere around Jerusalem for help in times of stress, the answer was to be found where it has been ever since the Jews left Egypt: in the presence of God. God's promise was to protect His people as long as they remained faithful to Him, and as a forgiving God, all that is necessary is for the people to return to Him. If they will simply believe in God's promise and trust in Him, His presence as the cornerstone will set everything true and straight again.

Just as God made his presence known in the ancient tabernacle in Jerusalem, God tabernacled with mankind in the Lord and Savior, Jesus Christ[38] whom both Paul and Peter established as the same cornerstone of the faith.[39] Because of this, many see no particular difference between the nature of the cornerstone in the Old and New testaments, noting that Isaiah was making a reference to the coming Messiah, Jesus Christ in this verse.

> *Isaiah 28:17. Judgment also will I lay to the line, and righteousness to the plummet: and the hail shall sweep away the refuge of lies, and the waters shall overflow the hiding place.*

Isaiah continues using the architectural design metaphor by adding the tools that are used to place the walls true to the cornerstone, the line and plumb. Just as the line and plum is used to true the walls, God's judgment is sure and true. The truth of God's judgment will be applied both on the surface where the lies are obvious, and in the subtle recesses where lies are hidden under any number of rationalizations and mistruths. Like a broom sweeping dust from the top of a stone, God's judgment will sweep away the lies and that which holds to them. Lies will not only be exposed and swept away, but their refuge will be exposed and removed also. Likewise, like a flood that fills every hole in its deluge, those deep hiding places where lies are hidden will be inundated and washed away. God's judgment will reveal and expunge every lie and rationalization that both Israel and Judah is depending upon as they reject God and seek to follow their own paths to utter destruction.

---

[38] John, Chapter 1.
[39] Ephesians 2:20. 1 Peter 2:6.

> *Isaiah 28:18. And your covenant with death shall be disannulled, and your agreement with hell shall not stand; when the overflowing scourge shall pass through, then ye shall be trodden down by it.*

Israel and Judah chose to place their trust in alliances with warring nations which, over the events of time, would result in their being swept away by the deluge of Assyrian and Babylonian invasions that would take place over the next century. Isaiah's prophesy would become both figuratively and literally fulfilled. When we read of the capture of Jerusalem by Nebuchadnezzar and his taking of thousands of captives, and we hear of the stories of Daniel, Shadrach, Meshach, and Abednego in Babylon we often fail to realize that their captivity served God's purpose as the faithful remnant was protected against the deluge of invasion, a deluge that totally wiped both Israel and Judah off of the map. The small population that remained behind in and around Jerusalem continued to rebel against Babylon and was routed by Babylonian forces, resulting in their exodus and assimilation to Egypt, quite the irony since it was out of Egypt that Israel was born as a nation and it was back into Egypt that it died.

> *Isaiah 28:19-20. From the time that it goeth forth it shall take you: for morning by morning shall it pass over, by day and by night: and it shall be a vexation only to understand the report. [20]For the bed is shorter than that a man can stretch himself on it: and the covering narrower than that he can wrap himself in it.*

When we place our trust in things of this world rather than in God, we will always find that the world will always fall short of our expectations. First of all, God is to be the authority in the life of the faithful, and as soon as we turn our back on Him, we assign that authority over us to other things. For example, we may think that the purchase of that bright and beautiful, expensive new car will make our life more pleasant, and then add a new boat, motorcycle and new kitchen appliances to the house that we can barely afford. As the debt load adds up, we are enslaved to debt payments, having no money which to honor God in our stewardship or meet the daily needs of life, needs that God has provided for, but we have squandered. When we surrender to such authorities we are, like the Hebrews, making alliances with that which is not of God, and consequently, we are making a pact with Sheol, a figurative reference to the depths of this world.

When Israel confidently made its pact with Damascus, it found itself allied with Judah's enemy when Damascus attacked Judah in its own attempts for conquest. Three years after the pact, Damascus itself was overrun by Assyria, nullifying any value to Israel that the pact had promised. Likewise, Judah made its alliance with Egypt. When Babylon threatened Judah, Egypt failed to honor its part of the alliance and had long before retreated from Nebuchadnezzar's advance, leaving Judah defenseless.

God's promise to provide for those who place their faith and trust in Him is sure. When we place our faith and trust in things of this world, we place them on things that are untrustworthy, and sometimes the results can be disastrous. When we place our trust for eternal security in this world, the results are eternally disastrous. The value of the things of this world will always fall short of our expectation when we come before God and the choices of our lives are judged.[40]

---

[40] Revelation, Chapter 20.

> ***Isaiah 28:21-22.*** *For the LORD shall rise up as in mount Perazim, he shall be wroth as in the valley of Gibeon, that he may do his work, his strange work; and bring to pass his act, his strange act. ²²Now therefore be ye not mockers, lest your bands be made strong: for I have heard from the Lord GOD of hosts a consumption, even determined upon the whole earth.*

Isaiah began and ended this passage with a reference to mockers. He proclaimed the kings of Israel and Judah to be mockers as they demonstrated the wickedness of leading the nations into apostasy and ultimate disaster as they removed the nations from God's hand of protection. After illustrating the consequences of such mockery both in fact and in fulfilled prophesy, Isaiah turns his reference from the kings to the peoples of the nations with an imperative to "**be ye not mockers**." How do we respond to this imperative? We find an answer by looking at the circumstance of Israel and Judah as they made a mockery of God in two areas: in their security, and in their practice.

We make a mockery of God when we place our eternal security in the things of this world: good works, religious practice, or any other endeavor that denies salvation by faith in God alone. Just as God demonstrated His presence in the Jerusalem tabernacle, described by Isaiah in the metaphor of the Cornerstone, God fully demonstrated His presence in the Messiah, Jesus who is the Cornerstone of all faith in God. Jesus paid the penalty for sin, for all of those who place their faith and trust in God, and it is only through that final act of atonement is salvation truly found. All truth is measured in Jesus. When we deny Jesus, we deny God, and when we deny God we make ourselves to be mockers. It is only when we place our faith and trust in God that the words of mockery are silenced.

We also make a mockery of God when we inordinately depend upon the things of this world. God desires to be your Lord, and to be so He must be Lord of all. A common cliché rings true: Jesus is Lord of all or He is not Lord at all. A king has both authority and possession over everything in His domain. For us to truly submit to the Lordship of Jesus Christ, we must trust all that we have to Him. In this we find a significant truth. It is not in our wealth that we find security: it is in the things that God has given us, including our wealth that truly belongs to Him, that our needs are met. If God is the Lord of our wealth, the decisions we make concerning it will always be made with prayer and consideration of God's will. This same principle applies to every facet of our lives. When we give back to God everything that He has given us He will "do His work" and "bring to pass His act."

Are you a mocker? Have you placed your trust into the things of this world? Have you given authority to things other than God, whether it be enslavement to things of this world or to people? A simpler question is this: Is Jesus the Lord of your entire life, and have you given everything to Him? It is only when we submit to God as our Savior and Lord that we will find ourselves free of the sin of mockery. When we place our trust in God we will also find that God is true to His promise that He made with Israel at Mt. Sinai: He will give us the land in which to live, including all that we need to live in it, and will protect and preserve us forever. That is a pretty good deal. Why would anyone refuse it?

> *Some trust in chariots, and some in horses: but we will remember the name of the LORD our God.* **Psalm 20:7**

Isaiah 29:13-16; 30:12-18.
Rejecting the Potter's Hand

"Oh, it was God's will." How many times have we heard those words spoken by someone who is trying to justify the reason or purpose behind an event that defies an explanation? One commentator[41] gave an example of a young man who chose to drive under the influence of alcohol and caused an accident that took the life of a mother and her two children. He stated, "I can't believe my drunk driving caused the deaths of ... Maybe this happened as God's will to make me straighten up my life." In this case the young man was employing blame shifting, refusing to accept responsibility for his own actions and in a likewise irresponsible manner, assigned the blame on God. This may be an extreme example, but the young man's way of thinking is one that many share: using blame shifting as a justification for doing things our own way and then assigning responsibility for the circumstances of our choices to God. It is obvious that God would not cause the death of a mother and her two children just to teach this arrogant young man a lesson. It is obvious that the young man caused the deadly accident and is accountable for his negligence and blatant disregard for the safety of others.

I once encountered a grieving mother who blurted out "Why did God kill my child?" A drunk driver had recently struck her

---

[41] Dunston, p 38.

daughter who was playing near the street. My answer was that God did not kill her child; an irresponsible drunken man did. I explained that God loves both her and her daughter, will give her comfort as she grieves, and He will hold the man accountable for his actions, as will the State of Tennessee who charged him with vehicular manslaughter.

It is easy for us to blame God for the consequences of man's sin. Romans 8:28 reminds us that God works all things for good, and in some circumstances some good is hard to find. In the first example the young man may have straightened up his life after the shock of his murderous behavior, but at what cost was this lesson learned? We are responsible for our own choices and the consequences that they may bring. To place blame on God is to behave at the height of arrogance and cowardice, while reducing the glory of God to little more than a blasphemous excuse. This is the testimony of one who is spiritually blinded by their own self-justification. This is also an example of the breaking of the third commandment concerning the taking of the name of the LORD in vain. To take the LORD's name in vain is to deny His power and purpose, a sin that is expressed at the very core of man's arrogance.

The practice of this sin can in of itself bring tremendous pain and loss to both the sinner and to the lives he/she affects. When that person has great responsibility, many people, as many as a nation can be affected. At the time of this writing if Isaiah, Hezekiah is sitting on the throne, serving as a vassal to his mighty Assyrian neighbors. This state of the nation of Israel came about because of Judah's continual choice to seek security in making alliances with its neighboring rival kingdoms. God promised to care for them if they would follow Him. Instead they rejected God, and like the young drunken driver, they are choosing to act in a manner that can only bring death and destruction.

Isaiah 29:13. *Wherefore the Lord said, Forasmuch as this people draw near me with their mouth, and with their lips do honour me, but have removed their heart far from me, and their fear toward me is taught by the precept of men:*

Isaiah has been describing the apostasy of the nation and the consequences that Judah will suffer because of it. The Judeans lay a claim to righteousness, and despise all others as being unrighteous. They defend their claim based upon their ancestral line to Abraham, and upon their adherence to the Law of Moses. However, Isaiah clearly indicates the hypocrisy of these claims. The Judeans claim godliness with their words, and repeat stated words that would bring honor to God. However, their spiritual blindness is revealed in their hypocrisy. Their hearts are far removed from God; they have no real love for God, nor do they have any real interest in Him. Instead, they have replaced the power of faith with a powerless religion of works, a religion that has been formulated by the works of men.

Where the Mosaic Law was intended by God to expose the sins of an ungodly lifestyle, the Jewish leadership used it as a book of law, a list of rules to be followed in order to obtain righteousness. This is the fallacy of all religions: righteousness cannot be obtained by the keeping of the law. Their hypocrisy is further illustrated in the simple fact that, even when they treat the Mosaic Law as a set of rules, no person can keep them all. The Law exposes all people as lawbreakers, and points to the need for a redeemer, the Messiah who will come and provide a way to find forgiveness. This is not what the Jewish leadership was teaching.

This form of hypocrisy is as prevalent today as it was during the years of the early church,[42] and as it was in the days of the Jewish kings.

> **Isaiah 29:14.** *Therefore, behold, I will proceed to do a marvellous work among this people, even a marvellous work and a wonder: for the wisdom of their wise men shall perish, and the understanding of their prudent men shall be hid.*

There is a consequence that comes with the rejection of God. Isaiah speaks of wisdom and understanding. When one rejects God, one rejects the only source of spiritual wisdom and understanding. God's Word is the only source of spiritual truth, and it is the complete source. God's Word is found as one reads the scripture and is open to the work of the Holy Spirit to guide one's understanding. The Judeans were reading scripture, but were not submitted to the LORD. Consequently, they came away with their own worldly interpretation that lacked true wisdom and understanding. The leadership, whom the people look to for wisdom (wise men) and understanding (prudent or learned men), is immersed in a religion of their own ideas, and have left God out of that religion. God is referred to by name only, and not by relationship or practice. Consequently, their wisdom and understanding is worldly, not godly. The truth is far from them.

> **Isaiah 29:15.** *Woe unto them that seek deep to hide their counsel from the LORD, and their works are in the dark, and they say, Who seeth us? and who knoweth us?*

---

[42] Matthew 15:9. This verse is quoted by Jesus.

"Woe" is the misery that comes from complete hopelessness. There is no eternal hope for any person who takes their rejection of God to their grave. The rejection of God by the religious leaders is so complete that they actually think that their scheming plans are being formed in secrecy. The forming of a military alliance with a pagan nation is clearly forbidden under the Mosaic Law, yet these leaders were in the process of negotiating with the Egyptian Pharaoh to form an alliance against the Assyrian threat. It is as though they think their plans are so well-hidden that even the LORD is not aware of what they are doing.

It may be hard for us to understand how the religious leaders could so easily reject the omnipresence and omniscience of God. Their view of God had long ago lost its wonder. In their hearts the God of Abraham had no more real power than the other pagan gods they venerated. It was easier for them to think that God resided in the Temple and was unaware and uninterested in things taking place outside of the holy place. The prophet Jonah demonstrated this when he thought he could escape God by traveling away from Israel.

> **Isaiah 29:16.** *Surely your turning of things upside down shall be esteemed as the potter's clay: for shall the work say of him that made it, He made me not? or shall the thing framed say of him that framed it, He had no understanding?*

Isaiah uses a metaphor similar to that of Jeremiah[43] and Paul[44] by comparing the nature of the potter and the nature of the clay that he uses to create a vessel. When we look at the two we find that all of the power to shape the vessel is held in the

---
[43] Jeremiah 18:1-6, et. al.
[44] Romans 9:19-21.

hands of the potter. It is the potter who drives the wheel and who uses his power to shape the clay. It is the potter who decides how the clay will be shaped. It is the potter who determines what the purpose of the finished clay vessel will be. In this exchange the clay itself has no power. It is simply dead material that the potter shapes into a form of his own liking. The clay has no ability to resist the potter except that it would be thrown away as refuse if it cannot be adequately molded by the potter.

God is the potter, and His people are the clay. God has the same authority and power over his creation that is illustrated in the potter and clay metaphor. To think that a lump of clay can shape the potter would be considered ridiculous by any rational man. Yet, these of whom Isaiah prophesies are attempting to do this very thing. They are "turning things upside-down" by usurping God's plan and purpose for Israel. They are forming their own god out of their application of the Law, and rejecting God who authored it. They are shaping their god by their own reasoning, developing an understanding that is based on their own logic. Rejecting the potter, they are attempting to form themselves into a shape of their own liking, one that is quite contrary to God's purpose for them.

We see much of this today in a world that has turned everything upside-down by accepting sin and rejecting godliness. People today form their own gods, their own systems of authority, based upon their own logic and worldly understanding. The world is consistent with Isaiah's testimony that many reject God as the creator, preferring to believe in a godless universe as they say "He made me not."

> **Isaiah 30:1.** *Woe to the rebellious children, saith the LORD, that take counsel, but not of me; and that cover with a covering, but not of my spirit, that they may add sin to sin:*

The LORD again reminds us of the woe that awaits those who reject Him and take up for themselves their own counsel. Their godless plans serve only to generate a sequence of one sin following another, a compounding of transgression that serves only to separate them from Himself. The Word of God has been clear from the very first time that God spoke to man that it is His counsel that we are to seek and not our own. When we limit ourselves to our own counsel we accomplish nothing greater than ourselves. Rather than follow the direction of the Spirit, we will follow the direction of our own sinful choices. Just as it takes a lie to cover a lie, sin is covered by more sin when we choose to reject God's plan and purpose.

> **Isaiah 30:2-3.** *That walk to go down into Egypt, and have not asked at my mouth; to strengthen themselves in the strength of Pharaoh, and to trust in the shadow of Egypt! ³Therefore shall the strength of Pharaoh be your shame, and the trust in the shadow of Egypt your confusion.*

When we seek the authorities of this world we will accomplish nothing greater than those authorities. Rather than rely on God in their time of stress, the Jewish leadership with King Hezekiah were secretly planning this alliance with Egypt, a force that they considered powerful enough to defend them against Assyria. Isaiah describes the simple truth that the strength of the Pharaoh is nothing more than a shadow. The authorities of this world are nothing more than a shadow when compared with the power of the Holy Spirit to work in it.

Note the characteristics of a shadow. It is simply the powerless image of something else. Judah is trusting in the power of a shadow when it looks to Egypt rather than trusting in God who has the true power to protect them.

> ***Isaiah 30:12-18.** Wherefore thus saith the Holy One of Israel, Because ye despise this word, and trust in oppression and perverseness, and stay thereon: ¹³Therefore this iniquity shall be to you as a breach ready to fall, swelling out in a high wall, whose breaking cometh suddenly at an instant. ¹⁴And he shall break it as the breaking of the potters' vessel that is broken in pieces; he shall not spare: so that there shall not be found in the bursting of it a sherd to take fire from the hearth, or to take water withal out of the pit.*

The nation will suffer the consequences of trusting in a shadow when they call upon a quiet and non-responsive Egypt in their time of need. The wall of protection that they think as Egypt is itself facing an imminent destruction. Egypt has always been considered the oppressor by the Jews and any negotiations with Egypt would be suspect because of Egypt's own desires for conquest. Egypt does not want to ally with Israel, it wants to destroy it. The Pharaoh is using deceit to gain the trust of Judah so that he can take advantage of that trust. However, as a shadow, the Pharaoh will never actually have any means to fulfill his desire for conquest.

Isaiah returns to the metaphor of the potter who, upon taking the finished vessel from the hearth finds it damaged. A breach in the pot renders the pot useless, so the potter simply breaks the pot into small pieces so that it can be easily discarded.

Note however, the "you" in verse 13 clearly refers to Judah as the pot, not Egypt. Like the useless pottery that is broken by the potter, it is Judah that will be broken into irreparable pieces by God because of its uselessness to Him.

> **Isaiah 29:15-18.** *[15]For thus saith the Lord GOD, the Holy One of Israel; In returning and rest shall ye be saved; in quietness and in confidence shall be your strength: and ye would not. [16]But ye said, No; for we will flee upon horses; therefore shall ye flee: and, We will ride upon the swift; therefore shall they that pursue you be swift. [17]One thousand shall flee at the rebuke of one; at the rebuke of five shall ye flee: till ye be left as a beacon upon the top of a mountain, and as an ensign on an hill.*

Isaiah referred to God as "The Holy One of Israel," a reminder that God is the one true God for Judah, the One with whom their covenant was established. In this passage Isaiah adds the words "Lord GOD" or "Sovereign LORD," a combination of Adonai and Yahweh that refers to God's sovereignty and His redemptive purpose. Isaiah prescribes the plan for hope for Judah, that they would return to Him, finding their confidence and strength in the Sovereign LORD.

However, the Jews refuse to rely on God when faced with Assyria. Their plan is established. The Jews did not tend to keep many horses. As a nomadic and agrarian culture there was little use for a horse. However, as a military conqueror, the Pharaoh had many horses. Their plan was simple: when the threat of Assyria is first heard they will ride swiftly to Egypt using Egyptian horses. Isaiah reveals the truth of their plan that, indeed they will find themselves fleeing the advancing

Assyrians, but without Egyptian help. They will flee in the thousands when the shadow of Egypt is found powerless.

> **Isaiah 29:18.** *And therefore will the LORD wait, that he may be gracious unto you, and therefore will he be exalted, that he may have mercy upon you: for the LORD is a God of judgment: blessed are all they that wait for him.*

Despite Judah's sin, God is waiting for the nation to repent and turn back to Him. The offer of restoration is never rescinded. God's very character is one of love and grace, and He is always waiting for the lost to return to Him. God is able to defend Judah against the Assyrian threat, and if the nation would simply repent of their apostasy, He will keep them safe.

How much suffering came to Judah because they refused the Hand of the Potter? How much suffering do we experience when we refuse the Hand of the Potter? It is good to know that the LORD is waiting like the father of the Prodigal to welcome His son home. As we face the threats of our lives, God's promise to empower us to stand against those threats is never rescinded. His promise of redemption is sure. As we look into our own lives we have the opportunity to identify those areas that we have not completely surrendered to God. These pockets of rebellion serve as our Egypt: that which we depend upon that has no more power than a shadow. However, the light of the Holy Spirit serves to expose and illuminate those shadows, flooding them with His love and His redemptive purpose. It is never too late to turn back to Him. Let us not suffer the fate of Judah who, as a nation, never did turn back to God, and depending upon worldly powers found itself destroyed by them. God is calling His people to turn from the authorities of this world and embrace Him fully.

Jesus is LORD of all. Consequently, He deserves that we give all to Him.

Isaiah 37:1-38.
Give Your Burdens to the LORD.

Have you ever found yourself in a truly difficult situation, one that brought great stress, one that brought with it confusion and grief as you are faced with more questions than answers? Certainly God has given us life, and many blessings, most of which we probably take for granted. However, the choices that we make in life have a dramatic impact on its circumstances. Likewise, the choices that others make often affect us in significant ways. Consequently, most of the circumstances of our lives are the results of choices that we and others have made, and sometimes the consequences of those choices are seemingly devastating. Sometimes the more difficult circumstances of life become burdensome, holding us down, and dragging us back like some great weight that is simply too heavy to bear. There are very few people who are spared the experiences that come with difficult circumstances, though our response to those circumstances is more a function of our attitude than the circumstances themselves.

Sometimes we carry great burdens. Single mothers usually must work outside the home, balancing the workload requirements of both the employer and the family, trying to completely fill the requirements of both when there is simply not enough time or resources to do so, and often without any assistance from others. Some are burdened by employment that creates stress in the home. Some are burdened by grievous illness that makes it difficult to simply get through a day. There are many who are victims of drug and alcohol abuse or of domestic violence. Many live in a state of poverty and destitution in nations that are ravaged by governments that seek power and despise their own people. Many are subjected to prejudice and hatred for their religious or ethnic status.

When we look at the circumstances that bring about the burdens that we carry in this life virtually all of these, with the exception of many health issues, find their roots in the choices we make. There is common thread that is woven through choices that cause grief, hurt and destruction, a thread that characterizes literally all loss and suffering: sin. There is no intent here to argue that all physical suffering is caused by sin, since it is clear in the teachings of Jesus and within any reliable biblical context that sickness is not an intrinsic punishment for sin. God did not plan on mankind to live on this earth forever, so death is sure, as is the common suffering that accompanies it. Still much sickness and physical suffering is caused directly by sinful choices when they involve activities that are clearly destructive including abuses that may involve substance, physical, psychological, ethical, or sexual abuse as well as the deliberate inflicting of injury on others.

In choosing us as His children, God gave us a better plan. An example of His plan is found in the covenant that God made with the tribe of Israel at Mount Sinai: God would forever provide both the land and the protection to remain in it as long as the people of the covenant placed their faith and trust in Him. Recorded in the books of Exodus, Kings and Chronicles are numerous examples of God's miraculous protection as He settled Israel in the areas around the Jordan River. However, it did not take long before the people forgot the covenant and turned away from faith in God to embrace the sinful culture of their secular and pagan neighbors. The people of God wanted to be more like the people of the world. They wanted a nation and a kingdom that was organized like the other nations. They desired to set up allegiances with their powerful neighbors rather than rely on God for their protection. When Samuel anointed Saul, the first King of Israel, he also prophesied that the Israelite kings would lead the people away from God, into bondage, and to their ultimate destruction. David followed Saul, and his son Solomon enslaved the Jews in his obsession to rebuild the nation. Solomon's son Rehoboam vowed to increase the bondage of the people, resulting in the split of the nation into a southern kingdom of Judah, (the tribe of Rehoboam), and the northern breakaway tribes of Israel.

From this point, the state of the two kingdoms went steadily downward. The northern nation of Israel never rose up a king who would lead the people to the Lord, but rather anointed a succession of ungodly kings who led the nation into pagan religious practices and engaged in the intrigue that existed between warring nations. In turning away from God, they broke the covenant at Sinai, removing themselves from God's hand of protection as Israel attempted to depend upon alliances with other kingdoms as their security. Israel's alliance with Damascus proved fruitless when that kingdom was overrun by Assyria in its drive for the conquest of other nations. Ten years later Assyria would thoroughly destroy Israel, taking its people captive and repopulating the land with peoples of other lands. The northern kingdom of Israel, as a nation, was never heard from again.

The southern nation of Judah remained after the destruction of Israel, in part because of God's protection over them that was provided to the remnant of faithful that remained there. However, that remnant had limited influence in the government and many of its kings, like those of Israel, led the nation away from God. King Hezekiah was a godly king who attempted to bring the nation back to God, but was faced with many obstacles that made his task nearly impossible.

Judah's situation was every bit as precarious as that of the northern nation of Israel in its latter years. Most of its kings had also led the nation away from God, but occasionally Judah would rise up a king who was faithful. As we approach the 37th chapter of the prophecy of Isaiah, the writer records events that took place under the reign of Hezekiah, one of the kings who sought to turn the nation back to God. However, Hezekiah was faced with a culture that made the task difficult. He was able to restore worship in the Jerusalem temple, but did not tear down the pagan altars on the mountaintops. Hence he did not banish pagan worship from the land. Hezekiah was not only faced with the dilemma of religious worship, but Assyria now had its sights on the conquest of Judea and had begun to make its move to put down Judea and the other nations that had rebelled against their domination by Assyria and its new king, Sennacherib (Se-NACK-a-reeb), son of Sargon II.

Sennacherib was himself quite a historian. He recorded detailed accounts of his conquests, naming the cities he destroyed and even the military tactics used his attacks. Though filled with his ego-centric viewpoint, these documents serve to give us some insight into the context of Hezekiah's dilemma, and their agreement with biblical accounts is encouraging. Sennacherib had advanced his army towards Jerusalem and was about to put the city to siege. He had just laid siege to and destroyed Lachish (la-KEESH), a city south of Jerusalem that was second only to Jerusalem as a fortress, and without an army or a foreign ally, Jerusalem's situation was grave. Sennacherib was currently stationed at Lachish.

> **Isaiah 37:1.** *And it came to pass, when King Hezekiah heard it, that he rent his clothes, and covered himself with sackcloth, and went into the house of the LORD.*

Prior to the attack, Sennacherib sent his cup-bearer (entitled, "Rabshakeh"[1] (RAB-shu-keh)) to Jerusalem with a plea to surrender. The Rabshakeh stated two points that are germane to our study: (1) Jerusalem would be destroyed if they do not surrender, and (2) Israel's God was using Assyria to punish the nation for its apostasy. The first point was one that Hezekiah could deal with. However, the second point brought Hezekiah to the point of mourning with sackcloth and ashes, and led him to go to the Jerusalem temple to seek the Lord.

How often do we wait until our situation is dire before we seek the Lord? How often do make choices for ourselves without inquiring of the Lord, and by so doing find ourselves seeking for an extraction from circumstances of our own making? It seems it is only when we cannot handle the situation ourselves that we finally go to the Lord with a plea for help. God's plan is that we place our faith and trust in Him continually, seeking His will in all of our decisions so that we do not get ourselves into such situations. This is where we find Israel: Assyria is poised to attack a defenseless Jerusalem and its King, Hezekiah is seeking the help of the Lord.

> **2 Kings 18:14-16.** *And Hezekiah king of Judah sent to the king of Assyria to Lachish, saying, I have offended; return from me: that which thou puttest on me will I bear. And the king of Assyria appointed unto Hezekiah king of Judah three hundred talents of silver and thirty talents of gold. [15]And Hezekiah gave him all the silver that was found in the house of*

> the LORD, and in the treasures of the king's house. ¹⁶At that time did Hezekiah cut off the gold from the doors of the temple of the LORD, and from the pillars which Hezekiah king of Judah had overlaid, and gave it to the king of Assyria.

In his surrender to Sennacherib, Hezekiah asked what Assyria would demand from him to deflect an attack. Sennacherib demanded from Hezekiah a deliberate return to his status as a vassal king over a conquered nation, and as an evidence of the dominance held by Assyria, demanded a huge tribute as a penalty for the rebellion of Judah and the surrounding tribes and nations that Hezekiah had led. Hezekiah was forced to pay the tribute from the temple treasures, a task that must have broken Hezekiah's heart.

Even when we turn to God in repentance, we may still find ourselves responsible for the consequences of our poor choices. We may suffer losses of health, losses of property, and losses of relationships with others. Sometimes these are losses that can never be regained. The loss for Hezekiah was grievous to him, as it would be he who would ransack the temple for Assyria of its items of value, items that Jerusalem's armies and its people had defended for years. These were goods that Hezekiah understood to be holy, belonging go God Himself. Consequently, Hezekiah's suffering was not only prompted by the threat of the Assyrian army, but also by the consequence that the threat had evoked. One can only imagine the burden that Hezekiah experienced when it was he who was robbing the temple under the authority of this Assyrian king. Hezekiah was so moved by this event that he called upon his prophet, Isaiah, for counsel.

Cyrus, and this Rabshakeh led the remnant of Judah back to Jerusalem.)

> **Isaiah 37:2-5.** *And he sent Eliakim, who was over the household, and Shebna the scribe, and the elders of the priests covered with sackcloth, unto Isaiah the prophet the son of Amoz. ³And they said unto him, Thus saith Hezekiah, This day is a day of trouble, and of rebuke, and of blasphemy: for the children are come to the birth, and there is not strength to bring forth. ⁴It may be the LORD thy God will hear the words of Rabshakeh, whom the king of Assyria his master hath sent to reproach the living God, and will reprove the words which the LORD thy God hath heard: wherefore lift up thy prayer for the remnant that is left. ⁵So the servants of king Hezekiah came to Isaiah.*

When Hezekiah observed his situation he came to realize that the Rabshakeh could have been correct. He describes the current days as ones of trouble, rebuke, and blasphemy. The trouble has come upon them as a result of their own apostasy, their own refusal to fully rely on God as their Provider and Savior, as they placed their trust instead upon their own ego-centric kings and in their alliances with other nations. They are now experiencing the rebuke of the Lord as their sin of apostasy has been exposed by the voice of a pagan neighbor, one to them who is a blasphemer. To hear such a rebuke from such a pagan, knowing that the content of the rebuke is true, makes for quite a wake-up call.

Often we experience such a rebuke when we allow things in our lives to get out of control, an allowance that comes from our self-dependence and our bent on prideful and self-centered choices. Sometimes it takes someone from outside of our comfort zone to expose the extent of our own apostasy, and by so doing cause us the embarrassment of seeing our sin exposed even to those outside that zone.

It is at times like these, when we find no other recourse that we finally enter the house of God (the tabernacle of the Holy Spirit that resides in the heart of every Christian) and come to God in prayer. Recognizing Isaiah as the Lord's prophet in Jerusalem, Hezekiah sent his leadership in a clear state of humility, to Isaiah requesting that he pray for the remnant of Judah that still remains.

> **Isaiah 37:6-7.** *And Isaiah said unto them, Thus shall ye say unto your master, Thus saith the LORD, Be not afraid of the words that thou hast heard, wherewith the servants of the king of Assyria have blasphemed me. [7]Behold, I will send a blast upon him, and he shall hear a rumour, and return to his own land; and I will cause him to fall by the sword in his own land.*

It had been a very long time in Israel since its king came before the Lord in true repentance. This was a king that truly desired to bring Judah back to God, though he had been frustrated in his attempts to do so. Hezekiah did not know what to pray, or what to pray for. He simply did what he could do to express his remorse and repentance for the situation that he and his predecessors had brought to Judah. Note that God did not rebuke Hezekiah, for the repentance in this king's heart was real and sincere. God did not require Hezekiah to perform some great work of faith in order to validate his sincerity, since God knows that Hezekiah's faith is sincere. Our human culture seeks to exact punishment for any act of wrong-doing, but God is characterized by His love and His grace, a grace that is given to all who place their faith and trust in Him. When we turn from our self-centered spirit and humbly come to him in true repentance (truly choosing to turn back to Him), God does not respond with rebuke and punishment, but rather with a demonstration of His love and His grace. Also, God is always true to his promise to take care of those who place their faith and trust in Him.

We do not have a record of the event through which Isaiah heard the word of the Lord, if there even was one. Isaiah, knowing God's heart, also was confident in his knowledge of God's will and purpose, and understanding God's response, he communicated this to Hezekiah's messengers: God accepts repentance without condition. God offers his gift of grace to all who turn to Him in Spirit and in truth. As a result of Hezekiah's repentance, God could fulfill His promise made at Mount Sinai when Hezekiah restored the covenant. As a testimony to the restored covenant, the people of Judah would see a miracle. God promised to deliver Jerusalem from the hand of Sennacherib, bringing destruction down on the Assyrian army, resulting in their retreat back to Assyria. Furthermore, Sennacherib would return home only to find his own death at the hands of Assyrians.

God would deliver Jerusalem. When Sennacherib would renew his threats against Judah, Hezekiah had a foundation of trust in God that would now deliver him from the desperate fear that he had experienced prior to Isaiah's prophesy. He also had confidence in the source of the strength of Israel: YAHWEH, the LORD, God.

Isaiah 37:8-13. *So Rabshakeh returned, and found the king of Assyria warring against Libnah: for he had heard that he was departed from Lachish. ⁹And he heard say concerning Tirhakah king of Ethiopia, He is come forth to make war with thee. And when he heard it, he sent messengers to Hezekiah, saying, ¹⁰Thus shall ye speak to Hezekiah king of Judah, saying, Let not thy God, in whom thou trustest, deceive thee, saying, Jerusalem shall not be given into the hand of the king of Assyria. ¹¹Behold, thou hast heard what the kings of Assyria have done to all lands by destroying them utterly; and shalt thou be delivered? ¹²Have the gods of the nations delivered them which my fathers have destroyed, as Gozan, and Haran, and Rezeph, and the children of Eden which were in Telassar? ¹³Where is the king of Hamath, and the king of Arphad, and the king of the city of Sepharvaim, Hena, and Ivah?*

Just as Israel had made a fruitless alliance with Damascus, Judah had sought to form a similar alliance with Egypt. Though, like Damascus, Egypt was not able to come to the aid of Judah, it was still not entirely omitted from the intrigue of the day. When Sennacherib had conquered Lachish, he turned to Libnah, a city closer to Jerusalem and not as fortified as Lachish. This was more of a mopping-up operation to the formidable Assyrian army. It was at this point that the king of Egypt was rumored to be finally coming to Jerusalem's defense, and Sennacherib had no interest in the delivery of any good news to Hezekiah when he is about to begin the siege. Instead of sending the Rabshakeh back with another speech, he wrote one himself, one to be delivered directly by messengers to Hezekiah, a letter that was written in his own words. This was a message meant to discourage the seemingly doomed king. The message was meant to cause Hezekiah to doubt the prophesy of Isaiah, and by so doing to doubt God's intent to deliver Jerusalem. The king of Assyria then goes on to list many of the pagan cities that were not protected by their gods, falling without exception to Sennacherib's advance. Jerusalem, like these, would also fall without the protection from the LORD that Hezekiah has suddenly embraced. As Hezekiah is being encouraged by the Lord through Isaiah, Sennacherib reminds Hezekiah that the kings of all these pagan cities are dead, and he is next.

When faced with a severe burden, how often do we hear the same messages, messages that are intended on inflaming our doubts? Often the voice of Sennacherib comes from our own heart rather than from that of a critic. We may recall the three friends of Job who counseled him to reject God, and his own wife who counseled him to "curse God and die." In our set of choices we also select those whose counsel we will openly receive, and sometimes those choices may be no wiser than the ones that placed us into a difficult situation in the first place. When we find ourselves burdened, and believe in our heart that God will be faithful to deliver us, we will still often be open to doubts, open to the discouraging words of others who do not share our newly sensitized faith and trust in God. This leaves us with a choice: to follow the Lord who we know is truth, or to follow our doubting heart and our doubting counsel who we know to be a lie.

> **Isaiah 37:14.** *And Hezekiah received the letter from the hand of the messengers, and read it: and Hezekiah went up unto the house of the LORD, and spread it before the LORD.*

No doubt, Hezekiah remembered the events of Israeli history, events that had described God's miraculous intervention to save His people in peril. The peril could be no greater for Jerusalem, so upon receiving the letter from Hezekiah instead of seeking an another alliance, instead of gathering together a conscripted army, instead of rattling his sabers in rebellion, Hezekiah took the letter into the temple, rolled it out on a low table (presumably meant as an altar), bringing it to the Lord as a matter of prayer. Why was this type of behavior not characteristic of Israel and Judah's kings? Why did it take the imminent demise of the city to finally bring Hezekiah to the point of bring his burdens to the Lord?

These are easy questions to pose, but our answers may smack of some hypocrisy when we ourselves tend to withhold our burdens from God's hand. The Apostle Peter was not unfamiliar with burdens, having experienced the lowest period of his life during the passion of Christ, yet Peter writes, "Cast all your anxiety on Him, because He cares for you".[45] Somehow our culture teaches us that God is there to help us when we are overpowered by our burdens, so we do not bring them to the Lord until we find them overpowering. Peter understood that we can bring all of our burdens to the Lord, and the word "all" is quite inclusive. We can, and should, bring the small burdens to God when they are still small, and give control of their management to God, seeking His will in the resolution of the conflict that those burdens bring. How did Hezekiah give this burden to God? We can see evidence of the king's methodology in his sincere prayer.

> **Isaiah 37:15-16.** *And Hezekiah prayed unto the LORD, saying, [16]O LORD of hosts, God of Israel, that dwellest between the cherubims,*

---

[45] 1 Peter 5:7.

> *thou art the God, even thou alone, of all the kingdoms of the earth: thou hast made heaven and earth.*

Hezekiah started his prayer with an humble recognition of the nature of God. We minimize God in our lives when we fail to yield our lives to Him, professing faith in God, but living by faith in our own works. When we truly recognize the awesome character of God, the God of Abraham, Isaac and Jacob, the God who created the universe, the God who came down to mankind to reveal His purpose and plan, we can only be humbled. A good start to the process of "burden relief" is to clearly know and accept the character of our God who can and will come to our aid and serve as the agent of our deliverance. Upon embracing this immense character of God, we can express our true humility by simply opening up the recesses of our heart and pray with this sincere confession, a confession of acknowledgement and praise.

Hezekiah first refers to God as the "LORD of hosts, the God of Israel". Both of these are references to the names used of God to refer to His covenant relationship with man. God is LORD, YAHWEH, the One God ("thou alone"), the provider and sustainer of life who has entered into a relationship with His creation through His covenant with Abraham, and with Israel at Mount Sinai. This is the same God to whom we pray. God has not changed.

Hezekiah's reference of the cherubim may be instructive. Isaiah is the only biblical writer to refer specifically to the creatures of heavenly worship referred to as cherubim, who had six wings: two for the covering of their eyes (representing their acknowledgement of God's unseeable glory), two for the covering of their feet (representing their humility), and two for flight. It is not until a faithful believer appropriates a true appreciation for the glory of God, and it is not until a true believer submits to God in humility, is the believer in a condition to truly fly, to truly serve God.

How often do we fly with all six wings, thinking that we can fly further, longer, and straighter without acknowledging God? By holding back that which is meant to worship God, we fly without His power. The cherubim serve as a metaphor, empowered to fully worship and serve God only after they have given to him a true sacrifice, the control of their own flight.

> **Isaiah 37:17.** *Incline thine ear, O LORD, and hear; open thine eyes, O LORD, and see: and hear all the words of Sennacherib, which hath sent to reproach the living God.*

Hezekiah then turned directly to the issue on his heart. He did not "beat around the bush" or hide his concerns behind a wall of rationalizations. As a sinful people none of us deserve the ear of God. When we come before God in true humility we will clearly recognize that we have no power to make God do what we want Him to do, but instead God will always perform His own will. The desire on Hezekiah's heart is the salvation of Judah from the hands of this brutal Assyrian king, so Hezekiah makes his desire clear as he notes the reproach of all that which is Godly that is represented in Sennacherib's attacks.

> **Isaiah 37:18-19.** *Of a truth, LORD, the kings of Assyria have laid waste all the nations, and their countries, ¹⁹And have cast their gods into the fire: for they were no gods, but the work of men's hands, wood and stone: therefore they have destroyed them.*

Hezekiah also opens up his heart to reveal his real fear: the destruction of the remnant of Judah. Assyria has laid waste to every nation it has attacked, and with no army to defend itself, there is no logical way that Judah can oppose its own inevitable demise. Hezekiah also notes the ineffectuality of pagan gods to protect their people, recognizing that they are not gods at all. He recognizes that God Jehovah is the only true God and unlike those made by the hands of Man, God can deliver the city from Assyria. Hezekiah's faith in God is so great that he has no doubt that God can deliver Judah using any method He would choose.

> **Isaiah 37:20.** *Now therefore, O LORD our God, save us from his hand, that all the kingdoms of the earth may know that thou art the LORD, even thou only.*

Hezekiah is asking for a miracle not unlike those experienced by a more faithful Israel of the past. He is also asking for a miracle that will show all of the nations that God is not a fabrication of wood or stone, but rather the true, living creator of the universe. Such a miracle would not only deliver Hezekiah from the burden he faces, but also would serve to glorify God. The witness of such a miracle could turn many people to God in faith, including those in Judea who still insist on worshipping the metal, wood, and stone idols of this pagan and secular world. Rather than ask for something that would serve only his own wants and desires, Hezekiah desires that this would also give glory to God.

Often we are not quite as open-minded in our own prayers as we form them from a laundry list of our own desires. Often when we pray together, we limit our prayers to our own desire that either we or those within whom we share a relationship are healed of some physical condition or disease, ignoring any other facet of God and His purpose for us. When we do this we are doing little more than trying to use God as a universal credit card to purchase for free a release from physical illness. Jesus said that our prayers are heard when we pray in His name:

> **John 14:13.** *And I will do whatever you ask in my name, so that the Son may bring glory to the Father.*

What does it mean to pray in His name? Some teach a "name-it-and-claim-it" theology that argues that any prayer that is sincerely asked of God will require His positive response based upon this promise. However, to ask in His name is to ask in a manner that is fully immersed in subjection to who Jesus is: Savior and Lord. A prayer that describes the desire of our own will, but not that of God, is not one that is in His name. Even at the Garden of Gethsemane, Jesus clearly acknowledged that the only answer to his prayer for release from the torture He was about to face would be consistent with the will of the Father.

> **Isaiah 37:21-35.** *Then Isaiah the son of Amoz sent unto Hezekiah, saying, Thus saith the LORD God of Israel, Whereas thou hast prayed to me against Sennacherib king of Assyria:* [22]*This is the word which the LORD hath spoken concerning him; The virgin, the daughter of Zion, hath despised thee, and laughed thee to scorn; the daughter of Jerusalem hath shaken her head at thee.* [23]*Whom hast thou reproached and blasphemed? and against whom hast thou exalted thy voice, and lifted up thine eyes on high? even against the Holy One of Israel.*

^{24}By thy servants hast thou reproached the Lord, and hast said, By the multitude of my chariots am I come up to the height of the mountains, to the sides of Lebanon; and I will cut down the tall cedars thereof, and the choice fir trees thereof: and I will enter into the height of his border, and the forest of his Carmel. ^{25}I have digged, and drunk water; and with the sole of my feet have I dried up all the rivers of the besieged places. ^{26}Hast thou not heard long ago, how I have done it; and of ancient times, that I have formed it? now have I brought it to pass, that thou shouldest be to lay waste defenced cities into ruinous heaps. ^{27}Therefore their inhabitants were of small power, they were dismayed and confounded: they were as the grass of the field, and as the green herb, as the grass on the housetops, and as corn blasted before it be grown up. ^{28}But I know thy abode, and thy going out, and thy coming in, and thy rage against me. ^{29}Because thy rage against me, and thy tumult, is come up into mine ears, therefore will I put my hook in thy nose, and my bridle in thy lips, and I will turn thee back by the way by which thou camest. ^{30}And this shall be a sign unto thee, Ye shall eat this year such as groweth of itself; and the second year that which springeth of the same: and in the third year sow ye, and reap, and plant vineyards, and eat the fruit thereof. ^{31}And the remnant that is escaped of the house of Judah shall again take root downward, and bear fruit upward: ^{32}For out of Jerusalem shall go forth

> *a remnant, and they that escape out of mount Zion: the zeal of the LORD of hosts shall do this.* ³³*Therefore thus saith the LORD concerning the king of Assyria, He shall not come into this city, nor shoot an arrow there, nor come before it with shields, nor cast a bank against it.* ³⁴*By the way that he came, by the same shall he return, and shall not come into this city, saith the LORD.* ³⁵*For I will defend this city to save it for mine own sake, and for my servant David's sake.*

It had been a long time since a king of a tribe of Israel had so sincerely approached the Lord for deliverance. God had promised deliverance to the faithful at Mount Sinai, a promise given to every individual who would place their faith and trust in Him. Israel and Judah had experienced the consequence of trying to live outside of the hand of God's protection, finding that their dependence upon their own armies or the armies of allied nations could not protect them. Despite the grievous apostasy of Judah that characterized its past, the repentance of faithful Hezekiah was accepted by God just as He accepts anyone who will repent and turn to Him.

Hezekiah heard the response of his prayer through another message from Isaiah. The LORD knows of the reproach and blasphemy of Sennacherib and his Assyrian nation, and the attack upon Judah, the children of God, is as an attack on Himself. We might characterize this as the response of a loving father to an unjust attack upon a beloved child. God promises to mount up like an army and destroy that by which Assyria holds its power including the resources that Assyria has besieged. God makes it clear that Sennacherib cannot escape the coming judgment since he cannot hide from God. Assyria will be tamed like a bull that is subjected to the nose hook and bridle, forced to follow the lead of the master as it is turned back from its plans of conquest. Instead of living off of the spoils of its conquests, Assyria will have to meet its own needs.

Furthermore, God makes a simple promise: Assyria will not have the opportunity to attack Jerusalem. Though the city stands defenseless against the Assyrian encampment of over 185,000 soldiers and support personnel at Libnah, only a few miles from the city wall, not a single arrow will fall on the city. God promised to deliver the city by His own power.

> **Isaiah 37:36-38.** *Then the angel of the LORD went forth, and smote in the camp of the Assyrians a hundred and fourscore and five thousand: and when they arose early in the morning, behold, they were all dead corpses. [37]So Sennacherib king of Assyria departed, and went and returned, and dwelt at Nineveh. [38]And it came to pass, as he was worshipping in the house of Nisroch his god, that Adrammelech and Sharezer his sons smote him with the sword; and they escaped into the land of Armenia: and Esarhaddon his son reigned in his stead.*

At some point after Isaiah's message was delivered to Hezekiah, Sennacherib experienced the devastating consequence of God's promise to protect Jerusalem. Where every other kingdom had fallen before his army like so many little dominoes in a row, Jerusalem would stand untouched. Sennacherib and his leadership awoke in the morning to find the army decimated by death in the night. The historian Sennacherib records the event in his annals, corroborating the biblical account of the sudden death of his army. Hezekiah put his trust in the Lord, while the Assyrian king had his trust in his own ability to place around himself an army and a leadership that could protect him. Now, Sennacherib found himself traveling back to Nineveh without his army, and without his circle of protectors. Soon afterward two of his sons killed him and fled the region, leaving a third son to serve as Assyria's king. Assyria would never again wield the power it had under Sargon II and Sennacherib. Instead, the power would soon shift over to a neighbor to the south, a neighbor who would again test the faith of Judah: Babylon and a king named Nebuchadnezzar. Mighty Assyria, the nation that destroyed Israel, found its demise at the hand of the LORD.

We see in this passage a dramatic illustration of the consequence of sin, the burden that sin brings, and the faithfulness of God to demonstrate His grace and love towards those who, even when immersed in the worst of circumstances, will repent of their sin and turn to God for help. We may ask, "Why did Israel and Judah so easily turn their backs on God and give up His promise of protection?" But, before we ask, we might look into our own hearts and ask the same question. Why do we so easily ignore God's will in our lives and build up for ourselves circumstances and burdens that bring us such stress and sorrow when God was there all the time? As we look at the stressors in our lives, let us evaluate their source. Are they the result of decisions that we have made outside of our truly seeking God's will? Are they decisions that were made by our own confidence to handle things our own way? Were they decisions that were clearly ungodly and unrepresentative of God's love? Is there conflict in our own lives that we have created through the expression of our own pride and self-will?

God's grace is amazing. Regardless of the depth we fall, He will always pick us up and deliver us. We may have to suffer the consequences of our choices, but as long as we place our faith and trust in Him, He will always be faithful to forgive. He will always be faithful to that simple promise: to provide a place for us, and to assure our place in it. For each who have placed their trust in Him, that place is eternal, and by His side. Just as Hezekiah placed the letters from Sennacherib on the altar of God, we have the opportunity to place on the altar those sins in our own lives that cause us such grief. Then, with a spirit of humility and repentance, let us ask God to take those sins from us and forgive us for our foolishness.

We all have a choice: either hold on to the heavy baggage of our lives, or let it go and give it to God. When we finally let go, we will begin to experience a greater peace and joy in our lives as we find our burdens lifted, replaced by God's love and grace that we are free to share with one another. What better choice is there?

Isaiah 38:1-8; 39:1-8.
The Folly of Human Choice

Have you ever gotten yourself in trouble by doing things that are simply unwise? Ok, so much for formal writing: have you ever done anything that is just, plain stoopid? We can all look back and be reminded of circumstances where we reacted or responded without an understanding or knowledge of all of the contexts of our decision, and came out of the experience having made the wrong choice, or exhibited the wrong behavior. The consequences of those decisions can be dramatic.

- When we react without thinking we can often hurt and insult others, damaging relationships.
- When we react without considering the consequences we can find ourselves immersed in those unexpected consequences.
- When we react without considering financial impact we can find ourselves inappropriately indebted.
- When we react without considering the context of the situation we can find ourselves missing out on what may have been a blessing.

It would seem that the forming of decisions has far more factors that would move us in the wrong direction than would lead us to a correct choice.

For most of us, the bulk of the choices we make have an impact on those around us, bringing change only to those in our close circle of relationships. However, there are some choices that we make that can change future generations until the end of the age. For example, in 1992 I moved my family from our Upstate New York home to the state of North Carolina following an employment opportunity after being laid off from my work. This was done while my children were in middle and high school. Consequently, both of my children have found spouses in North Carolina, and by so made North Carolina our home. The generations that follow are not the same generations that would have formed had we stayed in New York.

We often pay little notice to the significance of our decisions as we go through our daily routine. The Bible passage for this study draws from experience of Judah under the leadership of King Hezekiah around 704-703 B.C. Hezekiah, like the faithful today, had a true desire to follow the LORD. He brought worship back to the Jerusalem temple, worked to destroy the pagan worship centers in the region, and attempted to lead the nation under the authority of God.

However, Hezekiah was also a king, one who has a worldly position of authority with all of the riches and power that it brings. It was easy for Hezekiah to fall into self-sufficiency and consider the LORD only when circumstances were beyond his own control. This is probably similar to what leads the faithful today to make wrong choices. We tend to call on God only when circumstances are outside of our own control, as if we do not need God until all else fails.

1. GOD-DEPENDENCE IN THE TOUGH TIMES.

> **Isaiah 38:1.** *In those days was Hezekiah sick unto death. And Isaiah the prophet the son of Amoz came unto him, and said unto him, Thus saith the LORD, Set thine house in order: for thou shalt die, and not live.*

The scripture does not specifically identify Hezekiah's illness, though verse 21 indicates that his skin was affected. Such a visible sickness would have dramatic consequences for the king. The word leprosy was used in ancient times to refer to a collection of visible diseases, where today we tend to consider leprosy another name for Hansen's Disease, a treatable bacterial infection that destroys peripheral nerves and appears as scaly lesions on the skin. Such a disease would prevent the king from entering the temple, since the disease would render him unclean according to their religious tradition.

As the king, Hezekiah would have the power to respond to most situations with power and authority. However, he was powerless when faced with this disease, one that had the potential of taking his life. Though Hezekiah attempted to be a godly king, he tended to depend upon the prophet Isaiah to serve as his religious advisor rather than seek the LORD himself. However, this was one occasion where his power and authority meant nothing. Hezekiah sought the LORD.

> **Isaiah 38:2-3.** *Then Hezekiah turned his face toward the wall, and prayed unto the LORD, ³And said, Remember now, O LORD, I beseech thee, how I have walked before thee in truth and with a perfect heart, and have done that which is good in thy sight. And Hezekiah wept sore.*

We might note that Hezekiah did not go to the temple to pray, again indicating the visible nature of his ailment. The ancients equated sickness with sin, considering sickness to be a punishment from the gods for their unrighteous behavior. Consequently, it is no surprise that Hezekiah defends his position based upon his own impression of his righteousness. He tries to "remind" God of how good a person he is, and based upon his goodness he does not deserve the punishment he is receiving. He states that he has "walked in truth" with "a perfect heart." This is a testimony that many Christians might repeat, but we must always remember that no person is perfect; we all fall short of God's glory.[46] Hezekiah may have tried to walk in truth but his claim of goodness and perfection is certainly overstated. We find that Hezekiah, accustomed to the authority he has on the throne of Judah has transferred much of that authority into his own life, judging himself to be better than he truly is.

Hezekiah's sincerity is certainly evident by his passion as he is considering the possibility of dying. It may be interesting to note that the LORD, through Isaiah, did not give Hezekiah a time frame, and though the sense of the message might be immediate, God's timing is not necessarily our own. The instruction is for Hezekiah to put his house in order. At the time of this event Hezekiah has no heir, and his demise would end the Davidic line of kings, conceptually nullifying the promise that God made to David to preserve the line.

> **Isaiah 38:4-5.** *Then came the word of the LORD to Isaiah, saying, [5]Go, and say to Hezekiah, Thus saith the LORD, the God of David thy father, I have heard thy prayer, I*

---

[46] Romans 3:23.

> *have seen thy tears: behold, I will add unto thy days fifteen years.*

Can the circumstances of our lives change supernaturally through our obedience to prayer? Though some would argue that God's sovereignty disables Him from changing the unfolding of world events, the scriptural evidence testifies otherwise. The simplest example is the dramatic change that comes into one's life when they turn to God in faith. Their future that was doomed to separation from God is dramatically changed as the Holy Spirit works in their life to empower a relationship with God. God encouraged Hezekiah, through Isaiah, that He is quite aware of Hezekiah's circumstance and hears his prayers. the LORD assured Hezekiah that he would not immediately die from this disease. God would "add" fifteen years to his life. If God was telling Hezekiah that he would live another fifteen years after this event, then his son, Manasseh would be born three years later since the son took the throne at the age of twelve. Manasseh would be one of the most godless and brutal kings of Judah, having learned nothing of the faith of Hezekiah.

> **Isaiah 38:6-8.** *And I will deliver thee and this city out of the hand of the king of Assyria: and I will defend this city.*

Sennecherib was currently the king of Assyria and was threatening the city. Though Isaiah presents the chronology in a different order, the book of 2 Kings illustrates that the deliverance spoken of refers to the siege of Jerusalem that would take place under Sennecherib. The siege is described in chapter 37. Sennecherib sent his Rabshakeh (chief cupbearer) to Hezekiah, mocking the king, Judah, and Judah's God, and demanding surrender. While Sennecherib was still dealing with an uprising at Cush, he sent a letter to Hezekiah with a similar message. When Sennecherib finally brought his army to siege, the angel of the LORD swept through the army and in one night 186,000 soldiers died. Sennecherib returned to Assyria where he would later be killed by his sons.

2. SELF-DEPENDENCE IN THE GOOD TIMES.

> **Isaiah 39:1.** *At that time Merodach-baladan, the son of Baladan, king of Babylon, sent letters and a present to Hezekiah: for he had heard that he had been sick, and was recovered.*

Hezekiah had just experienced a series of miracles, given to Him by the LORD to encourage him and remind him of his dependency upon God and the power of God to do as He wills. This experience would have been a spiritual high, a seminal moment in his life where he experienced the voice and work of God first-hand. One might expect that Hezekiah would have a renewed commitment and would continue to seek God as he ruled over Judah.

Upon hearing of his sickness the king of Babylon sent emissaries to Hezekiah. The region of Babylon had broken away from the grip of Assyria and would continue to grow in power as the power of Assyria would decline. Judah offered two opportunities to Merodach-baladan. Merodach had the desire to conquer Judah, and his sending emissaries was a part of his plan to bring Judah under his own control. Also, the presence of the temple treasury was common knowledge. Merodach sought to know the actual content of the treasury and how the treasury was defended.

> **Isaiah 39:2.** *And Hezekiah was glad of them, and showed them the house of his precious things, the silver, and the gold, and the spices, and the precious ointment, and all the house of his armour, and all that was found in his treasures: there was nothing in his house, nor in all his dominion, that Hezekiah showed them not.*

One can learn a little bit about Hezekiah's true heart by the way he treated the group from Babylon. Having just experienced a miracle in his life, he went immediately back to the worldly context of a king. Hezekiah passed up an opportunity to testify to the greatness, mercy, and compassion of the LORD that he had just experienced. Had he simply given the ambassadors this message, the Babylonians would be reminded of the great God who has delivered them in the past, and consider the peril of attacking Judah. However, Hezekiah reacted to the visit like a proud head of state. He was "glad of them." He liked being treated as the king, and as the king of Judah Hezekiah had a lot to brag about. Because of his pride, he tried to show his greatness by the greatness of his wealth. The scripture reveals that Hezekiah gave Meredoch-baladan everything that he would need to plan his invasion.

What was the motivation behind Hezekiah's foolishness? We can see that Hezekiah's pride outweighed his sense of responsibility and the future consequences of his behavior. This seemingly innocent expression of pride would contribute greatly to the fall of Judah.

> **Isaiah 39:3-4.** *Then came Isaiah the prophet unto king Hezekiah, and said unto him, What said these men? and from whence came they unto thee? And Hezekiah said, They are come*

> *from a far country unto me, even from Babylon. ⁴Then said he, What have they seen in thine house? And Hezekiah answered, All that is in mine house have they seen: there is nothing among my treasures that I have not showed them.*

At the time of this event Babylon was not a major power in the region, so Hezekiah's prideful indiscretion seemed to him to be innocent enough. One can look into the heart of Hezekiah and feel the pride he felt in this visit from this "far country." He saw nothing wrong with his showing the treasuries to these visitors.

When we are faced with decisions it is easy to make the same mistake that Hezekiah made. Babylon was no threat to Hezekiah at this time, and he had no way of knowing what the future would bring. He did not consider the possibility that Babylon would be the next aggressor in the region. Their common enemy was Assyria, and Hezekiah sought to develop good relations with Babylon because of their plight. He was clearly placing his confidence in his treasury, and his confidence in an alliance with Babylon as an appropriate way to respond to the Assyrian threat. Hezekiah was trusting in the things of this world rather than the LORD for his protection.

3. OUR CHOICES REVEAL OUR TRUE HEART.

> **Isaiah 39:5-7.** *Then said Isaiah to Hezekiah, Hear the word of the LORD of hosts: ⁶Behold, the days come, that all that is in thine house, and that which thy fathers have laid up in store until this day, shall be carried to Babylon: nothing shall be left, saith the LORD. ⁷And of thy sons that shall issue from thee, which thou shalt beget, shall they take away;*

and they shall be eunuchs in the palace of the king of Babylon.

It would seem that this prophecy would come as a shock to Hezekiah. Isaiah uses the name, "Lord of Hosts," or "LORD Almighty," a name that refers to the infinite resources that God has to draw from in order to accomplish His purposes, purposes that include the defense of a godly nation. Where Hezekiah was proud of the resources of his treasury and his alliance with Babylon, he did not consider the far vaster resources that God would bring to bear to protect Judah if they would simply rely on Him.

Our foolish choices can have dramatic consequences. Hezekiah underestimated the ability or interest of Babylon to be a threat to him or the nation, giving them crucial information as they prepare their invasion. Isaiah revealed to Hezekiah some of the details of the consequence of his prideful actions. As Hezekiah had thought, Merodach-baladin would not invade Judah during his campaign against Assyria. However, Merodach's successor was the far more aggressive Nebuchadnezzar, and under his leadership he would invade Judah taking away all that is of value, including all of the treasures that Hezekiah had shown to the Babylonians. Furthermore, his own sons would be taken prisoner and castrated so that the Davidic line of kings would end. These are the devastating consequences of Hezekiah's prideful behavior: the fall of Judah, the nation that God called upon him to lead and protect.

One would think that Hezekiah would be as broken by this news as he was when he learned of the critical nature of his sickness. When the circumstance involved his own survival he wept bitterly and went to the LORD in prayer for help. One would expect that, now healed from his disease, Hezekiah would go immediately to the temple to pray to the LORD for his protection. He would announce to the people their need to repent and honor God who will deliver them from the Babylonian threat.

> **Isaiah 39:8.** *Then said Hezekiah to Isaiah, Good is the word of the LORD which thou hast spoken. He said moreover, For there shall be peace and truth in my days.*

Rather than show concern for the nation, Hezekiah was gladdened by Isaiah's prophecy. Abdicating any responsibility for the future of Judah, Hezekiah showed great pleasure that Judah would remain at peace during his lifetime. His lack of care for the future of the nation, or even the future of his own sons, who are not yet conceived, is amazing.

Hezekiah serves as a great example of one who lacks faith in God, but attempts to project it. He is expected, as the king of Judah, to lead the nation under the authority of God, so Hezekiah attempted to do so. He fully believed that he was righteous and perfect (verse 3), and believed that he was faithful. However, when we see the true heart of Hezekiah, we find a quite faithless individual.

Hezekiah believed in God, and had seen the miracles that God can do. Hezekiah believed the scriptures, and believed the words of Isaiah to be true. Hezekiah believed that God could extend his own life, and extend the life of the nation of Judah. The problem we find with Hezekiah's choices lie in one particular truth: Hezekiah believed in God, but did not place his faith and trust in Him. Much of our Christian culture today is made up of Hezekiahs – those who profess to be Christian but have never taken the necessary step of submitting fully to Him as both Saviour and LORD. Hezekiah had the Savior part down quite well. However, Hezekiah did not turn to God as his own LORD, submitting his life and his throne to the throne of God. He kept for himself those parts of his life that met his own needs for gratification and success.

We can learn from Hezekiah the perils of a profession of faith that lacks true commitment to the LORD. It is only when we profess God as our LORD will we experience the saving power of God. Without Him our choices are worldly, logical, and corruptible. Without Him we face a future and eternity that is devoid of His power and presence. Why would one choose to live the vain life of one as Hezekiah?

This passage gives to each of us an opportunity to look at the nature of our faith. Do we live for ourselves and seek God only when we "need" Him? Or, do we have a prayer-based relationship with Him that characterizes every moment of every day? If our testimony is the former, we have not turned our life over to God and may not have made the commitment to God that we profess. Let us never be satisfied to be a Hezekiah, but rather copy the character of Isaiah who had an open prayer life with God. Christians are called to imitate Jesus. Let us not imitate Hezekiah.

Isaiah 40:1-14.
Comfort in Times of Trouble

Troubles. There is probably no person who has ever lived who has not experienced times of significant difficulty and stress that come from an unlimited array of events and circumstances. One only needs to observe the front-page headlines of any newspaper to observe the more sensational events: people killed in bombings, deaths on our roadways, and senseless killings, each brining a wave of grief and mourning to the families of those who lost their lives. We learn of people who are suffering in destitution and poverty, suffering starvation and pestilence at the hands of nations whose leaders despise their own people. People suffer the effects of sickness and disease that are often debilitating, crushing the spirit of the one affected and bringing great stress to their loved ones. The mortality of man dictates that all will die, and we all hope that our own deaths will come without suffering. Now that I have reached that age where restaurants offer me discounts, I also find that much of the conversation that surrounds me involves health issues, as we deal with those concerns that surround the autumn of life. Thought the discomfort and inconvenience of illnesses do consume much of our attention in the latter years, much of our suffering throughout our lives comes from the consequences of our own ungodly choices and those of others.

How do people contend with such suffering and conflict? When all seems hopeless, where is a source of hope to be found?

> **Isaiah 40:1-2.** *Comfort ye, comfort ye my people, saith your God. ²Speak ye comfortably to Jerusalem, and cry unto her, that her warfare is accomplished, that her iniquity is pardoned: for she hath received of the LORD'S hand double for all her sins.*

The plight of ancient Judah engages many, if not all, of the stressors that we experience today. Historically, the most significant of these were the consequences of ungodly choices. In the first 39 chapters of his prophecy, Isaiah exposes the sin of Israel and Judah as each nation has turned its back on God, rejecting the covenant that the nation made with God following their emancipation from Egypt: a covenant to honor and obey God. In return for their obedience, God promised to protect them and keep them in the land that He would give them. The consequence of their choice was to lose their land, and hence their nation and their national identity when they exchanged God's protection for that of their warring neighbors. Those first 39 chapters describe the apostasy of the nations and the destruction that Israel and Judah will experience at the hands of Assyria and Babylon respectively. Isaiah's accuracy in his descriptions of the specific events that would transpire has led many to argue that the book is a historical record rather than a prophecy.

When we come to the 40th chapter of Isaiah, he has completed his disclosure of Israel and Judah's sin and its consequence. He now turns to a message that reaches beyond the events and their consequences as he addresses the core need of those who are immersed in the stress of their circumstances: hope.

Judah has witnessed the fall of the northern kingdom of Israel, yet has failed to learn from the event. They tended to think that they were invincible because of the presence of the Glory of God in the Jerusalem temple. They believed that to defeat Judah was to defeat God, and such a defeat would never happen. They had recently witnessed the miraculous failure of the Assyrian king, Sennacherib, in his attempt to besiege Jerusalem under the reign of the godly king, Hezekiah. However, the reign of godly kings would end and Judah, like Israel, would be destroyed. However, this destruction under Babylon's king Nebuchadnezzar would be different. Prior to its destruction, Nebuchadnezzar would take into captivity the faithful remnant of Jews, and would keep them together rather than disperse them as was done with the people of Israel by Assyria. After 30 years in captivity, Cyrus, the king of the combined Median and Persian empires would overwhelm Babylon, and take the region for his own. After another 40 years, Cyrus would allow the return of the Jews to Judah under the leadership of his Hebrew Rabshakeh (cupbearer), Nehemiah. Not only would Cyrus allow the return, but he also promised their protection as they traveled, and he provided much of the resource needed to rebuild the city. Nebuchadnezzar would not destroy Judah for yet another 100 years from the time that Isaiah writes, so we will see his prophecy to be quite amazing.

The message we find in Isaiah's 40th chapter is one of comfort. The command is given here that the people of Judah are to be comforted in their time of stress. Isaiah has already outlined the reason why Judah is suffering, and why Judah will be destroyed. However, Isaiah also assured the people that, true to God's promise at Mt. Sinai, the remnant would be preserved and protected. Though the warfare is still to come, it will come to an end. That end will also be the end of the consequence of their apostasy. We should probably note that though God allowed the destruction of Judah by Babylon, that destruction still resulted as a direct consequence of the decision of the Judean kings to place their trust in the untrustworthy neighboring nations instead of the Lord. It was those neighboring nations that destroyed them, and the influence of those nations would not last long. The consequence of their sin was profound, and Isaiah describes it as "double" that which the Lord would will. However, the punishment would be completed, and pardon would be received by those who trust God. Though Judah would suffer the consequence of their apostasy, they would not be abandoned by God, the time of suffering will come to an end, and they will find pardon.

> **Isaiah 40:3-5.** *The voice of him that crieth in the wilderness, Prepare ye the way of the LORD, make straight in the desert a highway for our God. ⁴Every valley shall be exalted, and every mountain and hill shall be made low: and the crooked shall be made straight, and the rough places plain: ⁵And the glory of the LORD shall be revealed, and all flesh shall see it together: for the mouth of the LORD hath spoken it.*

The Jews had just witnessed the destruction of Jerusalem and its temple. The most significant loss was in the removal of the Glory of God from the temple, something that the Jews never believed could happen. A return to Jerusalem could not be complete, at least in their own understanding, without the return of the LORD. Isaiah uses a well-understood ancient metaphor as he describes the return of the Lord to Jerusalem. It was a common practice for ancient kings to parade their gods into their new, conquered, lands. Though Cyrus was not yet in the historical picture, he was a master at this. The parade of their gods would be preceded by a preparation of the road where the king would pass. This could include renovation, construction, and any manner of preparation that would make the road passable. Borrowing from that cultural practice, Isaiah illustrates the return of the LORD to Jerusalem in a way they can understand. Not only will the return take place, it will come in a manner quite different than what Israel had experienced the first time. Though God had brought Israel on a quite direct pathway to the promised land from their bondage to the Egyptian pharaohs, their fearful refusal to enter resulted in another 40 years of wandering and warfare. The pathway of the LORD from Egypt to Canaan was anything but straight. This time the preparation would be so complete that even the mountains and valleys would be leveled to make the path straight. The return of the LORD would not be impeded by obstacles in the pathway, whether they be understood as wandering, warfare, or any other circumstances of resistance.

The prophecy was fulfilled when the Persian king Cyrus decreed the safe return of the Jews to Jerusalem. Whether their return was taken directly across the expanse of desert between Nineveh and Jerusalem or whether they traveled over the more passable northern route is unknown. However, the directness of the path is a more of a metaphor of a path that is traveled without resistance than it is a reference to a compass.

John the Baptist also drew from this metaphor as He announced the coming of the promised Messiah.[47] to Judah, claiming his own as the voice in the wilderness, and referring to Jesus as the LORD who is coming. John understood that his own ministry was to prepare the way for the LORD. Consequently, this message of Isaiah has a broad application as it refers to both the return of the LORD to Jerusalem in the emancipation of Judah from Persian captivity, as well as the emancipation of the faithful from the captivity of sin. One can easily see how the experience of the Jews in Assyria/Persia and their return to Jerusalem is a type of the separation from God that all people find as a consequence of their own sin and the emancipating power of Jesus' death on the cross that returns all of the faithful to God.

The first return would be a note in the historical record, described in the biblical accounts of Ezra and Nehemiah. The second return would change the historical context forever. All people of the earth would know of the return of the LORD, though most will still reject Him. Even calendar years throughout the world are based upon the return of the LORD in the birth of the Messiah. (Note that there is a drive by the liberal elite to rename B.C. and A.D. to BCE and CE, one that will probably be successful, in an attempt to further diminish the evidence of the coming of the Messiah. "Before Christ" and "Anno Domini", the "year of our LORD", will be replaced with "Before Common Era, and Common Era," simply another euphemism since the calendar will still rotate around the coming of the LORD. Indeed, all flesh will still "see it together."

Of course, Jesus promised that the end of this age would come with His return, a time when all flesh will see Him, a time when every knee will bow, and every tongue will confess that Jesus is LORD.

> **Isaiah 40:6-8.** *The voice said, Cry. And he said, What shall I cry? All flesh is grass, and all the goodliness thereof is as the flower of the field: [7]The grass withereth, the flower*

---

[47] John 1:23.

fadeth: because the spirit of the LORD bloweth upon it: surely the people is grass. ⁸The grass withereth, the flower fadeth: but the word of our God shall stand for ever.

Sometimes we put a great deal of stock in our own importance, or in the importance of the events of our day. All of the most important people, events and circumstances of this world are temporal, and their influence will pass. The Assyrian nation that destroyed Israel would soon diminish following Sennecherib's defeat at Jerusalem. Nebuchadnezzar's Babylon would soon fall to the Medo-Persians under Cyrus. The face of world circumstance is ever changing, and nothing ever lasts forever. However, there is one constant that is reliable: the Word of God stands unchanging forever. When we put our trust in things of this world, we place it on things that do not last. When we submit ourselves to the authorities of this world, we do so with authorities that will not last. This was a clear message to Israel and Judah who submitted themselves to worldly authorities rather than to God. God's promise of protection and preservation is offered to everyone who places their faith and trust in Him, and unlike every other influence of this world, God's promise will never change. God is eternal, and separate from the age of this creation, and in His eternity there is consequently no context for change. God will be standing at the end of this age exactly as He is now. His word will not change, and His word contains the whole of who He is, including His promises. We can be comforted to know that, regardless of how bad we think the circumstances of this world are, they will not last forever, and God will still be there.

It may be interesting to note that the "grass withers and the flowers fade because the Spirit of the Lord breathes upon it." The devolution of all that is in this world is in God's perfect plan. God does not plan that people would live forever, so the degradation of human health in latter years is in God's plan. However God's promise remains, that those who have placed their trust in Him will not be ultimately disappointed, but will find an eternal relationship with Him, a relationship that will stand with Him forever.

> **Isaiah 40:9-11.** *O Zion, that bringest good tidings, get thee up into the high mountain; O Jerusalem, that bringest good tidings, lift up thy voice with strength; lift it up, be not afraid; say unto the cities of Judah, Behold your God! [10]Behold, the Lord GOD will come with strong hand, and his arm shall rule for him: behold, his reward is with him, and his work before him. [11]He shall feed his flock like a shepherd: he shall gather the lambs with his arm, and carry them in his bosom, and shall gently lead those that are with young.*

Not only do we give great importance to the circumstances of our day, we also give them the power to discourage us. When we immerse ourselves in the satiating and gratifying world of self-pity, we can easily blind ourselves to the big picture: God is still on the throne, and His ultimate purposes will not be dissuaded by my petty complaints. The fact that God is always faithful to His promise is great news. Isaiah points out that this is news that is worthy of shouting from the mountaintops. Why do we need to shout, to "lift up thy voice with strength"? Sometimes it is hard to get our attention when our focus has been turned away from God's grace.

We might see a parallel in the Glory of God that appeared as a pillar of fire to the Israelites as they left Egypt. The sight of the pillar of cloud in the day, and the fire at night was a wonder to behold. When the shepherds witnessed the Glory of God at the annunciation they were struck with great wonder and fear. Likewise the Roman guards were struck with awe and fear when they witnessed the Glory of God at the tomb on Easter morning. That same pillar of fire stood over the tent of meeting and the Jerusalem temple for 1200 years. By the time that Judah was attacked by Babylon, the people did not even give notice to it any longer.

When we immerse ourselves in the issues of our own little world, it is easy to ignore the blessing that God has provided. Isaiah points out several of the comforting truths about God's continual presence in our lives:

1.) **"God will come with a strong hand."** He is greater than anything that this world has to offer. God is greater than the greatest of my worries. God is greater then the greatest of my sins. There is nothing in this world that can come between God and those he loves.[48]

2.) **"His arm shall rule ..."** As much as we give authority to the powers and principalities of this world, it is still God who is in control.

3.) **"His reward is with Him."** Despite all that the world can do to vex the life of the faithful, their reward is not with this world, but with an unchanging, faithful, and loving God.

4.) **"And His work ..."** God has a plan and purpose that transcends my circumstance. I may think that the consequences of a recently diagnosed medical condition are dramatic and debilitating, yet those circumstances do not overpower me when I understand that God has a plan that supersedes those circumstances. I will find the doors of

---

[48] Romans 8:38-39.

opportunity opened when it is His plan I follow, and not my own.

5.) **"He shall feed ..."** Much of the stress and chaos that is experienced in the life of many people is related to their diligence towards self-sufficiency. People work to make more money and accumulate more property with the assumption that there will be some point in time when that accumulation will bring security. However, that someday never comes. Our security is found in the LORD who has promised to take care of our needs. There is no need to fear that one's needs will not be met when one is fully faithful to the Lord. One who is faithful will not be slothful, so sufficient work and opportunity for work will be provided. If one cannot work, God provides.

6.) **"He shall gather ..."** God's ultimate plan is to bring to Himself all of those who place their faith in Him. This is a promise that is sure. It is a promised that is based upon God's unchangeable character.

7.) **"and He shall lead..."** We wander from God's plan when we, like the ancient Israelites, turn our back on God and follow the things of this world. We sometimes find the immediate sensual rewards of this world to be more attractive than an assurance of the future. We then make choices that are independent of God's plan and purpose for our lives and we find ourselves in a mess. Sometimes we will get to the point of asking where God is, or even blaming God for the mess we are in. God's promise is simple: He will lead those who will follow Him. We can turn from our bent for self-will and surrender to His will. When we do so, He promises to lead us.

> **Isaiah 40:12.** *Who hath measured the waters in the hollow of his hand, and meted out heaven with the span, and comprehended the*

> *dust of the earth in a measure, and weighed the mountains in scales, and the hills in a balance?*

Do we fail to appreciate the immensity of an infinite God? When we place our own limits on our understanding of God, we also limit what we think He can do in our lives. Isaiah illustrates the immensity of God in what he understands as the unfathomable dimensions of God's creation. With today's scientific scrutiny we can measure the amount of material in the earth, and we can measure the weight of the mountains. However, even science itself was not a field of study until A.D. 1400 to A.D. 1500. During the time of the writing of the scriptures, there simply was no science to draw from in order to answer Isaiah's questions. The ancients held in awe the immensity of the earth, while many today marvel at how small the world is. However, it is still difficult to grasp the immensity of this expanding universe as we gaze across millions of light years of space at far-away galaxies. Yet, God holds all of this creation in His own hand for His own pleasure. One cannot measure God by any scale that can be physically represented. When we truly begin to grasp how great God is, we can only begin to understand how God is sufficient to fulfill all of his promises to us.

> **Isaiah 40:13-14.** *Who hath directed the Spirit of the LORD, or being his counsellor hath taught him?* [14]*With whom took he counsel, and who instructed him, and taught him in the path of judgment, and taught him knowledge, and showed to him the way of understanding?*

Just as God cannot be measured by any physical means, His wisdom cannot be measured by any wisdom of man. Do we think we know better than God when we make choices that are based upon our own desires; when we clearly know that they are not in God's will? When we leave God out of our decision making, we are demonstrating that we consider our own wisdom greater than that of God. Isaiah asks the question, "what person has ever given counsel to God? Who taught to God His knowledge?" We might sometimes think that we can instruct God on the appropriate choices in our own lives, but such a position only demonstrates the depth of our own foolishness. Yet, it is in that foolishness that we often get ourselves into stressful or hurtful circumstances. However, the wisdom and understanding of God is still and always will be available to those who will trust in Him.

> **Isaiah 40:27-28.** *Why sayest thou, O Jacob, and speakest, O Israel, My way is hid from the LORD, and my judgment is passed over from my God? ²⁸Hast thou not known? hast thou not heard, that the everlasting God, the LORD, the Creator of the ends of the earth, fainteth not, neither is weary? there is no searching of his understanding.*

There are many who act as though they think that God is unaware and uninterested in the matters concerning their lives. Some teach that God is simply too "busy" to have time for us, and they may direct their prayers to the Virgin Mary or to a subset of those faithful Christians who have already gone to be with the Lord, a subset who may have a special status with the Lord because of their proven faithfulness and martyrdom. Such an argument may make sense from a standpoint of human logic, but it denies the true nature of God. While we may think that God is too busy for us, or that our way is hidden from Him while He looks elsewhere, we also agree that God is omniscient: He knows all. If God is omniscient, there is simply nothing that escapes His knowledge. There is no limit to God's understanding. There is no limit to God's knowledge of the details of our circumstances. Jesus taught His disciples to pray to the Father, and that same opportunity is offered to every disciple of Christ, to every believer. We cannot hide from God, and we cannot offer prayers that He cannot hear. To think we can do so is to deny His omniscience and place human limitations on Him.

Consequently, we can always be assured that, whatever the circumstances are in our lives, God always knows and God always cares.

We also understand that God is omnipotent: that His power is limitless. Unlike we who grow weary at the end of a busy day, God never tires, never sleeps, nor has need of sleep. God does not grow weary or distracted from His love for us. God is always faithful, always dependable.

> **Isaiah 40:29-31.** *He giveth power to the faint; and to them that have no might he increaseth strength. ³⁰Even the youths shall faint and be weary, and the young men shall utterly fall: ³¹But they that wait upon the LORD shall renew their strength; they shall mount up with wings as eagles; they shall run, and not be weary; and they shall walk, and not faint.*

From where do we draw strength in times of trouble? Isaiah has included in this chapter an in-depth discussion of the nature of God, a nature that demonstrates His faithfulness to those whom He loves. When we try to draw the power to overcome our circumstances either from ourselves or our own resources, we rob ourselves of the true source of power: God Himself.

There is a common child's chorus that states, "This little light of mine, I'm gonna let it shine!" The truth is, those who have placed their faith and trust in the LORD are the light of the world,[49] and that is no little light. God's light is the very Glory of God that holds the power that created this entire universe. That resource is available to every believer who places their faith and trust in Him. That power is engaged every time we turn to the LORD for our strength and for our help.

This passage contains one of the most often-quoted verses in the book of Isaiah. What does it mean to "wait upon the LORD"? The promise is simple: if we wait upon the LORD, our strength will be renewed and our "flight" will be restored. If we "wait upon the LORD" the promise is that we will be able to continue on without collapse, that we will have the strength to continue on when times seem too hard to do so. Some people will take the word "wait" from a single literal English use and understand it to mean that one is to simply rest, to sit down and do nothing. Such resting can renew strength, but it does little or nothing to provide us with the resource to overcome the troubles that impact our lives. The Hebrew text engages a deeper meaning to the word, "wait." It involves a trust in the Lord and a surrendering to Him that inspires one to submit to His will, following His lead instead of our own. There may be some form of waiting involved if it means to stop our head-long effort into solving our problems our own way and pause to listen to the Holy Spirit as He speaks to our hearts. It may be to wait quietly and listen to that still-small voice of the LORD that we so easily drown out with our own self-will.

When we continue in our attempt to overcome the many troubles of this world we can become exhausted and disillusioned. We may even find our situation beyond hope, much as those ancient Jews did who saw their doom at the

---

[49] Matthew 5:14-16.

hands of their warring neighbors. However, God's promise has never changed: if we turn to Him in faith, He will protect us and keep us secure in the land of His promise. Indeed, when we surrender our own self-will to Him and look to Him for our strength, we will find the true source of our sustenance, the true wisdom of His heart, and the meaning behind the issues of our lives. Why would we ever turn down such an offer of love?

Isaiah 42:1-7.
God's Missionary Plan.

What do you think of when you hear the words, "Foreign missions," "World Missions," or "Home Missions"? Many of us probably think of how the LORD called someone else who we do not know to some place we've never been to bring the gospel message to somebody we will never meet. We may have been programmed to think that the mission of spreading the message of God's love and purpose for mankind is someone else's task that we enable by our giving and by our prayers. We may have been trained that, by praying and giving, we have fulfilled God's purpose for us as He has called us to the mission.

Though praying and giving are essential to the mission, the call upon each Christian goes far beyond these two simple actions, driving to the very core of the Christian experience. As long as Christians are convinced that missions is someone else's calling, millions upon millions of people who live among faithful and dedicated Christians will fail to hear the gospel message in a way that they are given an opportunity to respond to it.

Perhaps it would be a good idea to provide a simple definition of this word, "missions." For the evangelical believer, "missions" as a noun refers to the task of sharing the gospel message with a lost world. As an active verb, it refers to the engagement of one's life in the variety of actions that will promote the gospel message everywhere from our own neighborhood to the far-reaches of the human community.

Why should Christians care deeply about missions? A heart that is open to the Holy Spirit is going to be open to the Holy Spirit's call to share God's true and unconditional love with the lost whom God seeks to save. God is at work in the world on a mission to bring people to himself through His Word and the testimony of the church. Only the unholy spirit would lead a faithful Christian to be apathetic to God's work. We find the scriptures full of imperatives for the faithful to be fully engaged in God's work, and the passages to follow give us some guidance on what it is that God wants to do through the lives of the faithful.

God wants to bless all nations

> **Genesis 12:1-3** *Now the LORD had said unto Abram, Get thee out of thy country, and from thy kindred, and from thy father's house, unto a land that I will show thee: ²And I will make of thee a great nation, and I will bless thee, and make thy name great; and thou shalt be a blessing: ³And I will bless them that bless thee, and curse him that curseth thee: and in thee shall all families of the earth be blessed.*

When a person truly responds to the call from God, the creator of the universe, that response is never trivial. Anything short of a radical life change is not a response at all. Genesis, chapter 12 describes call of Abraham by the LORD. We see through Abraham's experience an example of what happens when a person surrenders fully to the Lordship of God.

After the Great Flood, the world began to again deteriorate spiritually, illustrating man's inability to find true righteousness apart from God's intervention. At first, God exposed the pride of the people and scattered them to create a need for them to turn back to him.[50] Then he called Abram from Ur of the Chaldees to go to Canaan and to set into place His plan to bring the world to Himself.

Following God can lead us away from our natural comfort zone. God led Abraham to leave his native home and travel to an unknown land without any clear explanation of where he was to go, or why he was to go there. All that was left for Abraham was to choose obedience or disobedience.

By leaving the comfort zone of his home country Abraham would go to places with unfamiliar languages and customs, losing his position and security that he had come to know in his home in Ur. Abraham would also leave behind many of his day-to-day acquaintances and relationships. Also, he would be leaving the land of his father, giving up his claim to any inheritance. Following God can, and will be, a step of faith. However, that step comes with a promise from God.

What promises did God make to Abram?

- Abraham would become a great nation. That is, he would have many descendants. At the time of the call Abraham had no children.
- Abraham would be blessed, a reference to his coming position of fatherhood.
- Abraham's name would be great. Though going to a strange land, he again will be known, and will known as a leader. His would be a name that would be remembered.

---

[50] Genesis 11:1-9.

- Abraham would be a blessing (*berakah*) to the world.
- God would bless those who bless Abraham, curse those who curse him. That is, God promised to stand by Abraham through all of his relationships, both those who would be his friends and those who would be his enemies.

  Finally the kicker...
- Through Abraham the whole world would be blessed.

What did Abram have to do to receive this promise? All Abraham did was respond to God in obedience. Unlike the rest of the world that rejected God, Abraham had come to have faith in God, and through that faith, God could speak to Abraham and use Abraham for His own purpose. That purpose started by leaving behind the familiar territory of his homeland.

A key to understanding the promise is wrapped up in the word, "bless." Two forms of the word are used in these scriptures, and an understanding of these can help us to see God's purpose. What do you think of as being blessed? We might consider a blessing to have material possessions, physical beauty, or any other of the things that this world considers of value.)

> **John 10:10b.** *I am come that they might have life, and that they might have it more abundantly.*

God promises a life of abundance to those who, like Abraham, follow him. Consider how the beatitudes of Jesus' *Sermon on the Mount* describe blessing:

Matthew 5:3-9. *Blessed are the poor in spirit: for theirs is the kingdom of heaven.*
⁴Blessed are they that mourn: for they shall be comforted.
⁵Blessed are the meek: for they shall inherit the earth.
⁶Blessed are they which do hunger and thirst after righteousness: for they shall be filled.
⁷Blessed are the merciful: for they shall obtain mercy.
⁸Blessed are the pure in heart: for they shall see God.
⁹Blessed are the peacemakers: for they shall be called the children of God.

Jesus describes several of the blessings of an abundant life, including inclusion in the kingdom of heaven, comforting in times of mourning, inheriting the earth, having needs fulfilled, finding true mercy, seeing God, and acceptance as sons of God. Observation of these verses reveals what the true blessing is salvation. Each of the beatitudes first describes an attribute, or fruit, of an obedient and faithful Christian and then describes the blessing received as a result of that behavior. A blessing, as used in the scripture, comes from only one source: God, Himself. The blessing is given only to those who follow God in obedience. We cannot separate the word "blessing" from the word "inheritance" because, as an inheritance is given by a father to his son, the blessing from God is given to his children.

God promised Abram to bless him, and used the illustration of his fatherhood to make Abram understand. However, there was a problem concerning Abram's fatherhood. He and Sarai were about 75 years old at the time of the call, and they had no children at the time. However, Sarah would later have a son, Isaac. when Abraham was about 100 years of age. Abraham and Sarah waited for 25 years and during that time they doubted God's promise for a blessing.

Abraham understood God's blessing as coming through his son. What would be difficult to understand is that God promised that the whole world would be blessed, or receive the inheritance, through Abram. This blessing took place over a thousand years later when Jesus was born, a descendent of Abraham, and through Jesus, the whole world would be able to receive the inheritance that was promised to Abraham. Abraham may not have understood this, but many of the prophets did.

When one surrenders their life to the LORD, and become available to be used by Him for His purpose, there is no limit to what God can do in that individual's life. It is certainly possible that a faithful individual can be used of God to bless people far beyond their local circle of relationships, touching people all around the world.

God wants to bring justice to all nations (Isaiah 42:1-4)

> **Isaiah 42:1-4.** *Behold my servant, whom I uphold; mine elect, in whom my soul delighteth; I have put my spirit upon him: he shall bring forth judgment to the Gentiles. ²He shall not cry, nor lift up, nor cause his voice to be heard in the street. ³A bruised reed shall he not break, and the smoking flax shall he not quench: he shall bring forth judgment unto truth. ⁴He shall not fail nor be discouraged, till he have set judgment in the earth: and the isles shall wait for his law.*

This was written by Isaiah about 800 years after God's promise to Abraham. Except for a small cave and surrounding ground, Abram never personally received the land of God's promise. Following a famine, he went to Egypt where his descendants languished for about 400 years before reentering the promised land. God then brought them out of Egypt in a spectacular demonstration of His presence in the Shekinah Glory, the Holy Fire that led them through the wilderness to the promised land, and remained over the tabernacle for another 400 years. By the time of Isaiah's writing, the nation had again turned away from God, and God would use the Babylonians and Assyrians to conquer and take Isaac's descendants into captivity, removing them from the promised land because of their apostasy.

However, God spoke to several prophets during this time of decline, including Ezekiel, Malachi, Jeremiah, and Isaiah. Look at the servant described in Isaiah 42:1. Most commentators use the context of the book's other uses of the servant to conclude that this servant is the chosen people, the children of Isaac. However, I do not agree because the conclusions of verse 1 do not describe Israel. God did not delight in Israel's disobedience; as a nation, Israel did not accept God's Spirit, and the nation did not bring justice (or judgment) upon the nations. Israel was never in a position of the judge over all nations. However, this is an appropriate description of the Messiah, Jesus, a descendent of Abraham, and hence, a descendent of Israel.

God said that it would be through Abraham that the world would be blessed and Jesus came through Abraham. The next verses describe the servant and His purpose.

Jesus is the One who has the authority and purpose to judge all of the nations. Salvation comes by faith in God, and the righteousness that salvation brings comes only through the shed blood of Jesus Christ. Only through Jesus will any person come to God in righteousness. Consequently, it is through Jesus, not through the historical nation of Israel that judgment is found.

Some of the character of the one who would bring justice is described. When we look at this character we find that the purpose of judgment is not to bring down condemnation, but rather, to bring about redemption and restoration.

1. His message would be gentle. It would not be a message of rebellion.
2. He would not serve to bring any hurt to the physically or socially downtrodden.
3. He would not serve to bring any hurt to the spiritually downtrodden.
4. He would not serve to quench the spirit of those who are weak in the faith.
5. His message would be one of truth, exposing sin, and rewarding obedience.
6. His ministry would not fail.

These same attributes are descriptive for one who is submitted to God's call to share His love with this lost world. By sharing God's love, one shares the one Truth, exposing sin in gentleness with a purpose of redemption rather than condemnation.

God wants to give light to all nations

Isaiah 42:5-7 *Thus saith God the LORD, he that created the heavens, and stretched them out; he that spread forth the earth, and that which cometh out of it; he that giveth breath unto the people upon it, and spirit to them that walk therein: ⁶I the LORD have called thee in righteousness, and will hold thine hand, and will keep thee, and give thee for a covenant of the people, for a light of the Gentiles; ⁷To open the blind eyes, to bring out the prisoners from the prison, and them that sit in darkness out of the prison house.*

These verses describe the mission of the Servant: to give light to all nations. The purpose of light, as described in these verses is to reveal truth. God often uses light as a metaphor for His presence. God revealed Himself to Moses in the burning bush, about 400 years after God's promise to Abraham. He then revealed himself in the pillar of fire that led Israel out of Egypt to the promised land. The pillar of fire remained over the tabernacle for 400 years until David's reign, and over Solomon's temple for 400 years until Israel and Judah were taken into captivity by the Assyrians and Babylonians. At that point the pillar of fire left the temple, described by Ezekiel's prophecy. Then, for another 400 years, the fire was gone. The pillar of fire never again descended into the Temple on the day of the Holy of Holies and consumed the sacrifice. The Glory was Gone.

However, the glory returned when…

> **Luke 2:8-11.** *… there were in the same country shepherds abiding in the field,*

> *keeping watch over their flock by night. ⁹And, lo, the angel of the Lord came upon them, and the glory of the Lord shone round about them: and they were sore afraid. ¹⁰And the angel said unto them, Fear not: for, behold, I bring you good tidings of great joy, which shall be to all people. ¹¹For unto you is born this day in the city of David a Saviour, which is Christ the Lord.*

The Shekinah Glory returned, and lit up the hillside, frightening and amazing the shepherds. I am convinced that all of the would-be scholars who have tried to explain the Christmas star are way off the mark. They argue that the "star" was an alignment of planets, an atmospheric anomaly that reflected the sun in the upper atmosphere, and other speculative physical geological and cosmological arguments. The scripture states that the star led the wise men to where the baby lay, just as the pillar of fire led Israel to the promised land. It is the opinion of this author that the Christmas Star was none other than the Shekinah Glory of God: His presence demonstrated through the supernatural use of natural light; the pillar of fire.

> **John 8:12** *Then spake Jesus again unto them, saying, I am the light of the world: he that followeth me shall not walk in darkness, but shall have the light of life.*

Jesus states that the purpose of the light is to provide life to those who walk in darkness. The source of that light is Jesus Christ, and He would remain that source until the crucifixion:

> **John 9:5** *As long as I am in the world, I am the light of the world.*

When Christ died, the light was apparently extinguished. However, it was necessary that Jesus die, not only for the atoning act for our sins, but also that as a physical man, he cannot reach the whole world. Jesus only reached a few hundred people. However, the light again returned. When was that?

> **Acts 2:1-4.** *And when the day of Pentecost was fully come, they were all with one accord in one place. ²And suddenly there came a sound from heaven as of a rushing mighty wind, and it filled all the house where they were sitting. ³And there appeared unto them cloven tongues like as of fire, and it sat upon each of them. ⁴And they were all filled with the Holy Ghost, and began to speak with other tongues, as the Spirit gave them utterance..*

The same light from God that we see through the scriptures came to rest on the faithful believers, those who received the Holy Spirit. This is consistent with Jesus' prophecy that followed the beatitudes in Matt. 5:14-16:

> **Matt 5:14-16** *"You are the light of the world. A city that is set on an hill cannot be hid. ¹⁵Neither do men light a candle, and put it under a bushel, but on a candlestick; and it giveth light unto all that are in the house. ¹⁶Let your light so shine before men, that they may see your good works, and glorify your Father which is in heaven.*

God's mission has always been to save mankind. Before God created the universe and mankind, He had planned that his truth would spread throughout the world. His plan is that this would be don by empowering the faithful with His Holy Spirit. How are Christians to take the message of the gospel to all of the corners of the earth? By letting their light shine. Prior to His ascension, Jesus described how that light would shine throughout the entire world.

> **Acts 1:8.** *But ye shall receive power, after that the Holy Ghost is come upon you: and ye shall be witnesses unto me both in Jerusalem, and in all Judaea, and in Samaria, and unto the uttermost part of the earth.*

Jesus commands that the faithful would serve as witnesses to Him. Jesus describes four people groups, a list that is inclusive of all people, consistent with the unconditional nature of *agape* love. The global impact of the mission starts at home, among those whom you already have established relationships, your Jerusalem. It also includes the command to share God's love with those in the region outside of your daily commute, your Judea. It also includes the command to share God's love with those who you have difficulty loving, your Samaria. Finally, the impact of each individual's Christian ministry is to reach to the ends of the earth.

Fulfilling the mission starts with your sharing your love, through the power of the Holy Spirit with those around you without condition or reservation. It culminates with the sharing of God's love around the world. How is this done?

(1) **Pray.** Pray for those to take the gospel message to places where we cannot go. Pray for the lost in each of these four people groups. Pray for a heart that is obedient to God's call to be part of His mission purpose.

(2) **Learn.** Learn about the needs of people in each of this four people groups. An obedient heart will be a heart that loves people as God's loves them, and will seek to know the needs of others so that they can be prayed for and supported in any way possible.

(3) **Give.** Support missions financially. It is impossible for every Christian to visit every corner of the earth to share God's love. However, God does call Christians to go, and He calls upon other Christians to support them. This support is necessary, tangible, and the responsibility of each Christian.

(4) **Go.** Become directly involved in mission work. Every Christian should have a personal evangelism ministry, one that takes advantage of one's existing relationships and existing interests. An obedient heart is a willing heart, one who is willing to step outside of their comfort zone when God calls. Any Christian can travel across the street, across this nation or across the world on mission. You can volunteer for a mission project, or trip, or prepare materials and resources for use on the mission field.

Isaiah 44:1-22.
Who (or What) Is Your God?

Have you ever given much thought about the basic priorities in your life and their ranking of importance? If you were to take a blank piece of paper and write on it the 20 or 30 most important things in life, you would probably list things like God, church, family, job, etc. If asked to place them in an order of priority, you would probably be able to do so with little difficulty. When we are unable to keep those important issues in life in their prioritized order, conflict and stress arises.

The conflict is created by a mix-up of authorities. When we give priority to things in our lives, it is very easy to give them authority over us, that is, we become their servants. For example, when one is enticed to purchase a new car, the purchase is usually done with the bank's money, placing the buyer in debt. Add to that automobile mortgage a house mortgage and credit card debt and the buyer is now under the authority of those loans. They buyer can no longer use that money for discretionary spending, and it most likely diminishes or eliminates stewardship. A job can be so engaging that the employee neglects spending precious time with his/her children. One may enjoy fishing to the point that family is neglected. A pastor can become so engaged in his ministry that his own family is neglected.

These are all examples of mixed-up authorities where one gives more authority a lesser influence than to one of greater importance, such as the family. Such cho-ices diminish the quality of our relationships with each other and with the LORD.

> **Isaiah 44:1-2.** *Yet now hear, O Jacob my servant; and Israel, whom I have chosen: ²Thus saith the LORD that made thee, and formed thee from the womb, which will help thee; Fear not, O Jacob, my servant; and thou, Jesurun, whom I have chosen.*

How easy is it for us to forget where we have come from? One of the basic beliefs of the Christian faith is the Lordship of Christ. Jesus is the Messiah, the creator, for without Him, nothing was made, and He dwelt among us.[51] God created us for relationship with Him. We were not randomly formed from some primordial soup that happened to be struck by a lightening bolt. God created all that is. Having created man, God states through Isaiah that this creation was for a purpose, so that those who put their trust in Him would have a relationship with Him. This is by God's choice, a basic character of His love and grace. Because of His nature, God has chosen to bless those who place their faith and trust in the One who created them, the LORD. Faith in God is faith in Christ. The two cannot be separated, for they are One God.

We get so busy with the structure of authorities we accept in our lives, that we often forget the significance of the One Authority who loves us and cares for us every moment of every day. We forget the one to whom we can be continually praying as we thank Him for every daily blessing, both seen and unseen. We forget to include Him in our daily decision making,

---

[51] John 1:1-16.

reserving God for the "Big" decisions, and ignoring Him in those that characterize the routine of our lives.

> **Isaiah 44:3-4.** *For I will pour water upon him that is thirsty, and floods upon the dry ground: I will pour my spirit upon thy seed, and my blessing upon thine offspring:* [4]*And they shall spring up as among the grass, as willows by the water courses.*

The atheist observes the rain and can provide a very convincing and accurate account of how this rain came from changes in the heating of the earth surface due to its rotation as moisture is moved around in a repeating cycle of evaporation and condensation. No God is necessary for this to happen, at least in the perspective of the atheist. The child of God agrees with the physics but also recognizes the One who set all this in motion and His purpose behind it. Isaiah's prophecy reminds us of God's promise to continually provide for the basic needs of those who trust Him. Using the metaphor of rain as it brings life to the grass to describe the life that He gives to those of faith who, like the grass, are empowered to spring up and blossom. Furthermore, a willow "by the water courses" is continually fed with a replenishing supply of water, providing the resource needed to grow unimpeded, springing up to full blossom and full maturity.

Ancient literature referred to flowing water as "living water" (e.g. John 4:10,11; 7:38). Just as water brings life to what would otherwise be dead grass, God's Holy Spirit brings life to what would otherwise be a dead spirit in the heart of man. Without the life giving water of the Spirit, one is separated from God, failing to experience that living water, satisfied instead with the dead water of the authorities of this world. However, when one receives the living water of the Spirit of God, they shall "spring up" like the tree by the river, maturing in their love of the LORD and bearing much fruit.

Is it possible to be rooted by the river, yet not partake of its nourishment? The tree flourishes because of its continual intake of life-giving water. However, a tree that is next to it, a tree that is diseased may not be able to draw the water through its roots, withers, and dies. We have a choice as to whether to accept the living water that God provides. God "pours" His Spirit upon those who He has chosen, those who trust in Him, yet what have we employed as "umbrellas" to deflect that which God has intended for us? And, what have we employed that distracts us from the realization that the Spirit is even there?

> **Isaiah 44:5.** *One shall say, I am the LORD'S; and another shall call himself by the name of Jacob; and another shall subscribe with his hand unto the LORD, and surname himself by the name of Israel.*

When we fail to fully embrace the relationship that God has planned for us, we tend to identify ourselves with worldly authorities. In this verse we see three ways people identify themselves with a righteousness that cannot save. Though some do identify themselves with the LORD, most do not. And many of those who make a profession of faith in God have not fully placed themselves under His Lordship. Instead, they identify with other groups. (1) Those who identify with the name of Jacob are those who profess righteousness based upon their ancestry. They depend upon God's acceptance of the faith of Abraham for their own righteousness while they reject God in their hearts. (2) Others identify themselves by their good works, striving hard to live a life that is righteous and godly, yet with none of the power, none of the living water, none of the Spirit of God in their hearts to empower their effort.

(3) Others simply place their trust in their identification with the church, often with churches that teach that salvation comes from membership at birth or by conversion, not by a profession of faith.

All three of these positions reject the nature of God and His purpose of the redemption of man from their sin. All three of these positions place their trust in things other than God: heritage, good works, and association. God is speaking through Isaiah to send a message of restoration, to cause us to look back to our roots, our real roots for the One who created us, for the One who can provide a real solution for our unrighteousness.

> **Isaiah 44:6.** *Thus saith the LORD the King of Israel, and his redeemer the LORD of hosts; I am the first, and I am the last; and beside me there is no God.*

Many of us have probably often seen printed evidence of the cliché "God is my Co-Pilot." It was a popular slogan for automobile bumper stickers in the 1980s and 1990s. Those who ascribe to the three previous errors would gladly and confidently embrace this thought. It sounds godly to include God in our daily activity, as He co-pilots our life. However, such a position trivializes God, and keeps us in the pilot's seat. God is God, not me. He is the One and Only God that exists. There are no others. For us to give such authority to any other spirit, creature, or creation is to dishonor and reject the One God who truly loves us, and who truly impacts our lives. It is the LORD who is the King of Israel, the authority over all who place their trust in Him. It is the LORD who is the redeemer, the One who has bought us back from the authority of this world.

This word, "redeemer" is significant to the understanding of this passage, particularly to those who read in the original language. A redeemer was one who paid the debt for another who could not pay it themselves. It would be a redeemer who would purchase the freedom of one who sold himself into slavery. It would be a redeemer who would buy back the land that was lost to debt, restoring it to the family. Only God can save us from the separation from Him that sin demands, simply because it is a debt that we cannot pay. No manner of ancestry can make us pure, perfect and righteous. No manner of good works can make us pure, perfect, and righteous. No manner of identity with a church group can make us pure, perfect and righteous. It is only by God's grace that righteousness can be found, when God chose to accept as righteous those who place their faith in Him. Though the sin-debt still had to be paid, God paid that debt Himself, hence He is the One Redeemer. We were redeemed by His descent from heaven in the life of the Messiah, Jesus Christ, who paid the debt at Calvary. The debt is paid. God is the One and Only God who truly provides both for our needs and for our salvation. There simply is no other, and there simply is no other way of righteousness. God is the first and last. He is before all others who would come, and He will remain when all others have withered and died.

> **Isaiah 44:7-8.** *And who, as I, shall call, and shall declare it, and set it in order for me, since I appointed the ancient people? and the things that are coming, and shall come, let them show unto them. ⁸Fear ye not, neither be afraid: have not I told thee from that time, and have declared it? ye are even my witnesses. Is there a God beside me? yea, there is no God; I know not any.*

Despite of our likely agreement of the truths of this prophecy, we often fail to live like we really rely on them. We appropriate for ourselves other authorities than God, ones that we can fabricate and control ourselves. We do this despite the continual testimony and evidence that there is only One God. God has shown Himself to us through His relationships with Adam, Noah, Abraham, and Moses when, through each one, God reiterated His plan for salvation: the redemption of those who place their faith and trust in Him, and Him alone. All of the evidence we have seen through the history of man points to the faithfulness of God and the unfaithfulness of man and man's inventions. Why are we so much more comfortable placing our trust in things of this world? Why do we so quickly submit ourselves to worldly influences rather than to God?

> **Isaiah 44:9-11.** *They that make a graven image are all of them vanity; and their delectable things shall not profit; and they are their own witnesses; they see not, nor know; that they may be ashamed. [10]Who hath formed a god, or molten a graven image that is profitable for nothing? [11]Behold, all his fellows shall be ashamed: and the workmen, they are of men: let them all be gathered together, let them stand up; yet they shall fear, and they shall be ashamed together.*

All of the things that we create that we give honor and authority to have no power to bring us closer to the God who would save us. We tend to be an iconic people, easily impressed with created things. I was once blessed to see "up close and personal" the Pieta, Michelangelo's sculptural depiction of His impression of the image of Mary the Mother of Christ as she held the dead body of Jesus immediately following His crucifixion. It was certainly the most incredible creation of man that I have ever observed. As I studied the sculpture, I first was drawn to remember and appreciate what God did as He served as my redeemer and how He is worthy to be my LORD. However, upon closer inspection I started to see mid 15th-century culture rather than what I would expect from a first-century image. These were two attractive Italians. I started to note more 15th-century influence when a woman next to me caught my attention, drawing me away from the sculpture to the people, and I found the people to be as amazing as the sculpture. People were worshiping the sculpture.

A missionary once told me of his purchase of a large, ornate, hand-made image of an alligator that he proudly displayed in the living room of his jungle home. Neighbors were doubly impressed and would return to his house to see his alligator. Soon they brought friends. Then they brought gifts to the alligator. At this the missionary realized that these people were worshiping the alligator. The missionary immediately discarded the icon.

We may not worship sculptures or icons, but the worship I see of college sports teams by Christians is equally obvious. People who are too "reserved" to shout praises to the LORD lose themselves in shouting for the team of their choice. Manufacturers put chrome on motorcycles for a reason: people love to look at things that are bright and shiny. Likewise, you will see glitter embedded in the paint of that bass boat at your local sports store. The number of little gods that creep into our experience is almost endless. They all serve only one purpose: to distract us from our focus on the One God. None of these things has the power to redeem us. None of these provides us with the sun, rain, and resources of nature. None of these can fill that hole in our heart that is reserved for God's Spirit alone.

> **Isaiah 44:12.** *The smith with the tongs both worketh in the coals, and fashioneth it with hammers, and worketh it with the strength of his arms: yea, he is hungry, and his strength faileth: he drinketh no water, and is faint.*

The icons that we give such authority to are all made by man. Michelangelo was a superbly skilled and talented artisan, but he is still a man, full of man's flaws and sins. He is still weak and mortal as any man. What sense does it make to worship something that was simply fabricated by the hands of a weak and sinful man?

> **Isaiah 44:13-17.** *The carpenter stretcheth out his rule; he marketh it out with a line; he fitteth it with planes, and he marketh it out with the compass, and maketh it after the figure of a man, according to the beauty of a man; that it may remain in the house. 14He heweth him down cedars, and taketh the cypress and the oak, which he strengtheneth for himself among the trees of the forest: he planteth an ash, and the rain doth nourish it. 15Then shall it be for a man to burn: for he will take thereof, and warm himself; yea, he kindleth it, and baketh bread; yea, he maketh a god, and worshippeth it; he maketh it a graven image, and falleth down thereto. 16He burneth part thereof in the fire; with part thereof he eateth flesh; he roasteth roast, and is satisfied: yea, he warmeth himself, and saith, Aha, I am warm, I have seen the fire: 17And the residue thereof he maketh a god, even his graven image: he falleth down unto*

> *it, and worshippeth it, and prayeth unto it, and saith, Deliver me; for thou art my god.*

We see in this description of the carpenter the futility of his ways. We might, at first, think that this is a ridiculous response for a person to have to an item that he made himself. However, this is not so far fetched. Imagine a modern carpenter who spends a year to two years making an outstanding and beautiful piece of furniture that he will show in his own home. Upon completion he looks upon it with pride. He cannot help himself from taking a deep sigh each time he passes it. When friends visit, the first thing they are introduced to is his new piece of furniture. If one of the grandchildren should threaten to scratch it, that child is banished from the room. This piece of furniture has become a god.

The most popular television entertainment today surrounds programs where "normal" people are granted great rewards and gifts, whether it be Survivor, *The Great Race*, *Extreme Makeover: Home Edition*, *American Idol*, or *Deal or No Deal*. They all play to the greed of the audience as the players vicariously play out a fantasy. We place ourselves into the experience of those on stage as we dream about winning that million dollars or receiving that home that is more appropriate for "the rich and famous." The ogling of these rewards is a form of worship. Again, our focus from what is real and valuable is replaced by a fantasy. When the television show is over, we have not been fed, we have not been clothed. We have wasted an hour or more staring at a box that displays images and sounds, and have accomplished nothing. Even the television, when it draws us away from worship, work, and ministry becomes a god.

This passage illustrates how even the intrinsic material, the wood, has no value. That which is not used in the fabrication process is waste, a waste that has no value to the carpenter. The furniture is made from the same wood, and is therefore intrinsically of no more value than the discarded wood. It is the carpenter who anoints the object with a blessing of its authority. It is we who assign god-status to worthless things.

In ancient pagan cultures this same anointing of created gods was a common and accepted religious practice, one that drew them away from their covenant with God. Ultimately, their penchant for chasing worldly gods led to their destruction. Chasing after worldly gods distracts us and defeats us. We find no strength in them. We find no redemption in them. From them we only find separation from God, and all that serves only to separate us from Him is sin.

> **Isaiah 44:18-20.** *They have not known nor understood: for he hath shut their eyes, that they cannot see; and their hearts, that they cannot understand. [19]And none considereth in his heart, neither is there knowledge nor understanding to say, I have burned part of it in the fire; yea, also I have baken bread upon the coals thereof; I have roasted flesh, and eaten it: and shall I make the residue thereof an abomination? shall I fall down to the stock of a tree? [20]He feedeth on ashes: a deceived heart hath turned him aside, that he cannot deliver his soul, nor say, Is there not a lie in my right hand?*

It may be instructive to note that this penchant for giving authority to worldly gods is not an act of open rebellion against God Himself. These are simply acts of ignorance. The carpenter who has elevated his new piece of furniture to a position of centrality in the home has no idea of what he has done. If one were to tell him he was worshiping his furniture, his response would be utter denial. Salvation comes from faith in God, and in Him alone. If one does not know this, how can they help but look in other places? Without a knowledge of the gospel, people are left to search for God wherever they can find Him. All people search for God, for we are created in His image as spiritual beings, so all are without excuse who have failed to place their faith in Him (Rom. 1). This places the responsibility on the people of faith to focus their energies in two areas. First it is important to recognize the impact of gods on members of the family of faith. It is the same ignorance that inspires pagans to worship valueless things that causes Christians to fail to recognize the authority they are giving to those same things. Christians are just as apt to fail to recognize that the thing they hold in their "right hand" is a lie. (Note the right hand is a metaphor for the works that represent a person's identity.) Second, there is a responsibility assigned to every Christian to share God's love with those who are lost, looking for and seizing opportunities to share the gospel so that this ignorance can be dispelled. Unless the lost hear the gospel, how are they to learn it, and how can they learn it if those who know the truth are silent? (Romans 10:14-15).

> **Isaiah 44:21-22.** *Remember these, O Jacob and Israel; for thou art my servant: I have formed thee; thou art my servant: O Israel, thou shalt not be forgotten of me. ²²I have blotted out, as a thick cloud, thy transgressions, and, as a cloud, thy sins: return unto me; for I have redeemed thee.*

Let us never forget who our God truly is. It is He who formed us, and it is only He whom we serve. Even though we fall away and chase after the things of this world, God never forgets us.

This is particularly true for those who have placed their trust in God, because their sin can no longer separate them from God. However, continued sin still diminishes or even overwhelms any daily relationship with God. Isaiah reminds us that God is the One who is faithful, and is still there. We are being called to turn from our chasing after the things of this world and return to Him, and to Him alone.

As you look at the priorities of your life, which of these have become little gods? Which of these are taking away from your expression of praise and worship of the LORD? Which of these are taking away from your ability to minister in His name? Which of these are diminishing your ability to honor God with your stewardship? Which of these are diminishing your ability to give your all to God?

The answers to these questions are instructive. Make a list, and check it twice. Then, pray about crossing out some of those gods as you act on your true belief that Jesus is LORD, for if He is not LORD of all, He is not LORD at all.

Isaiah 45:1-13.
God's Works Through His People

God's plan for His people is not subject to the vagaries of man's choices. In fact, often the opposite is true: God leads people to obedience to Him and works through the hearts and hands of people to accomplish His purposes. During the years that ancient Israel was approaching its demise due to its escalating apostasy, there was a great need for God to encourage and direct His people. The remnant of faithful had diminished in number and influence and would ultimately survive the impending destruction of their nation. However, this would only take place through the action of two pagan kings: Nebuchadnezzar of Babylon and Cyrus of Persia, each of whom heard from God and responded.

As we investigate this passage it would be instructive to first note who Cyrus is. Recall that Isaiah's prophesy was written about 100-150 years before the southern nation of Judah was destroyed by the nation of Babylon under Nebuchadnezzar. Cyrus was a Persian king who successfully led the combined armies of the Medes and Persians against Babylon shortly after Babylon destroyed Judah. Consequently it is about 200 years between the writing of Isaiah and the reign of Cyrus, leading many to conclude that the writings of Isaiah were actually written after the Babylonian exile. However, historical and contextual evidence clearly places the ministry of Isaiah at the earlier date.

Isaiah 45:1-2. *Thus saith the LORD to his anointed, to Cyrus, whose right hand I have holden, to subdue nations before him; and I will loose the loins of kings, to open before him the two leaved gates; and the gates shall not be shut; [2] I will go before thee, and make the crooked places straight: I will break in pieces the gates of brass, and cut in sunder the bars of iron:*

The Persian king, Cyrus was extremely successful in his military conquests. Note, written two centuries before, Isaiah notes by name that Cyrus' successes came at the hand of God. The "right" hand symbolized an individual's power, and God states that it is He who holds Cyrus' power so that the nations would fall before him. The LORD did, indeed, grant Cyrus a wide kingdom, reaching from central Egypt through southern Greece. Some of the kingdoms conquered by Cyrus included the Asiatics, Arabians, Assyrians, Babylonians, Bactrians, Cappodocians, Carians, Cilicians, Cyprians, Egyptians, Greeks, Indians, Lydians, Maryandines, Paphloagonians, Phoenicians, Phrygians, Saciens, Syrians, and others.[52]

The two leaved gates refer to the bronze gates of Babylon. The defeat of Babylon by Cyrus is recorded in Daniel, chapter 5 and mirrors Ezekiel's prophecy. Cyrus lead the Meads and Persians against the city in 539 B.C. only to find its surrogate king Belshazzar distracted by a feast and its true king waging conflicts elsewhere to the North. The Persians diverted the flow of the Euphrates into a swamp, lowering the water level enough to march their army under the river gates to the city's

---

[52] Xenophon

gates of brass, only to find them open. No defense was raised against the advance of Cyrus' armies. The LORD simply gave Babylon to the Persian king much like He gave Jericho to Joshua.

> **Isaiah 45:3-4.** *And I will give thee the treasures of darkness, and hidden riches of secret places, that thou mayest know that I, the LORD, which call thee by thy name, am the God of Israel. ⁴For Jacob my servant's sake, and Israel mine elect, I have even called thee by thy name: I have surnamed thee, though thou hast not known me.*

First, God is making it clear to Cyrus, through the two-centuries old prophecy of Isaiah, that God provided the city and its treasures, including its idols and secret stores, to Cyrus. The previous kings, Nebuchadnezzar, Nabonidus, and Belshazzar had held the remnant of Judah captive. Having completely conquered the region that included the area of Canaan, there was no political advantage to keeping the Judeans in Babylon, so it would be Cyrus who would have the opportunity to free the remnant from bondage. Consequently, it was for the remnant that God would choose and "anoint" this pagan Persian king.

God also makes it clear to Cyrus that He knows him by name, having been called by name through Isaiah's writing, even though Cyrus does not know God. Meeting Cyrus at his point of need, God communicates to Cyrus a little about the One who has given him such a great nation.

> **Isaiah 45:5-7.** *I am the LORD, and there is none else, there is no God beside me: I girded thee, though thou hast not known me: ⁶That they may know from the rising of the sun, and*

> *from the west, that there is none beside me. I am the LORD, and there is none else. ⁷I form the light, and create darkness: I make peace, and create evil: I the LORD do all these things.*

Like so many of the pagan nations, Persia was polytheistic. The Persians believed in a pantheon of Gods including two important and opposing deities: one a god of good (Ahura-mazda who created light) and a god of evil (Angra-mainya who created darkness). God is the creator and LORD of all, both good and evil, for evil is simply a perversion of that which is good.

Where the Persians had a god for every physical event, God communicates directly to Cyrus, through Isaiah, that He is the only one and true God, and it is He who has strengthened Cyrus. The pagans believed that their gods were responsive to them through their actions, God states that his blessing of Cyrus is one-sided: Cyrus did not perform any rite of worship or any other action to warrant God's good favor.

Why did God do this? First, God stated that he is using Cyrus for the sake of Jacob, a reference to the remnant of Israel that is being held captive during Cyrus' reign. Second, God is revealing himself to Cyrus so that He might use this Persian king for His own purpose. By granting Cyrus a wide area of conquest, the Persian reign would bring a period of peace to the entire region, providing an opportunity for the remnant to safely return to Jerusalem. Also by revealing Himself and His purpose to this Persian King, Cyrus will have the opportunity to share this truth with his nation that now encompasses the nations that had previously vexed Judah and Israel. For the first time, the pagan nations would hear from their own King a testimony of the reality of the one true God, the God of Abraham, Isaac, and Jacob.

> **Isaiah 45:8.** *Drop down, ye heavens, from above, and let the skies pour down righteousness: let the earth open, and let them bring forth salvation, and let righteousness spring up together; I the LORD have created it.*

Where the Persians would worship a god of rain in an effort to obtain it, God simply speaks and the rains fall. The Persians place great effort in their worship of their fertility Gods in an effort to realize a fruitful harvest of man, beast, and field. However, God simply speaks, and all the earth brings forth life. Furthermore, the gift of life that comes simply from God's will includes both physical and spiritual blessing as God is the creator of life, and the author of righteousness. All of Cyrus' gods are simply mythical creations of man's creative mind, whereas the LORD God is the true God, and the One who created all things.

It is notable that Isaiah makes use of the covenant name for God, as God refers to Himself as LORD, YAHWEH, God who was the Word that became flesh and dwelt among us, Jesus Christ.[53] This is one of the many places in the Old Testament where we find reference to the work of the pre-incarnate Christ, the LORD.

> **Isaiah 45:9-10.** *Woe unto him that striveth with his Maker! Let the potsherd strive with the potsherds of the earth. Shall the clay say to him that fashioneth it, What makest thou? or thy work, He hath no hands? ¹⁰Woe unto him that saith unto his father, What begettest*

---
[53] John 1:1-16.

thou? or to the woman, What hast thou brought forth?

God then reveals to Cyrus the foolishness with which one denies God. He repeats the metaphor of the potter and the clay as He notes the foolishness that is demonstrated by the discarded pieces of pottery who deny the existence of a potter.[54] His advice to the pottery shards is for them to spend their time with similar profit by pitching their battle against the other stones that they share with the trodden walkway. The potter's vision and his fingerprints are all over the pottery, so to deny Him is ridiculous. Furthermore, just as the potter made the completed pot, He has the ability to destroy it and scatter it among the potsherds. One is treading in dangerous territory when one denies his creator.

Since we are observing Hebrew poetry, Isaiah uses this form to illustrate a second metaphor to repeat the same concept, but in a more personal way. One would be completely foolish to deny that they were brought into this world through a mother and father. To do so is to turn to one's one father or mother and declare, "you did not beget me." This is what man is doing when he rejects God, denying His true status as the Creator, and by so doing denying His rightful position as LORD.

Israel denied God in this way when they turned from Him to the pagan gods of the world culture in which they were immersed. Society still does the same thing today in many different ways. One way is to dedicate one's self to any god other than YAHWEH, the LORD. Most of the world religions and cults lead people into this subtle, but deadly, error. Others deny God as they place authority in idols such as a career, the

---

[54] Isaiah 30:12, ff.

possessions of this world, power and influence, or submit to any other authority other than God.

Isaiah has twice used the phrase, "woe to them,"[55] to illustrate the dramatically dangerous state of those who reject God in favor of the pagan gods of this world. The woe is true and dramatic as it refers to the judgment that comes upon all who reject the Lordship of God in this life: a final and eternal rejection by the Lord when this life experience ends. God has promised an eternal relationship with those who turn to Him in faith, and has promised eternal separation for those who have chosen that separation.

> **Isaiah 45:11.** *Thus saith the LORD, the Holy One of Israel, and his Maker, Ask me of things to come concerning my sons, and concerning the work of my hands command ye me.*

The LORD gives to those who are hearing Isaiah's prophesy a rhetorical question. First He describes the nature of His own character, as the true God, the true LORD it is He who is the God of Abraham, Isaac, and Jacob, the Holy One of Israel. Furthermore it is He who created Israel. Having created mankind, and having created Israel it is God's opportunity and right to lead and direct Israel in the manner of His wisdom and choosing. If God chooses to free Israel from their exile through the edicts of a pagan king, what person can stand with God and challenge His methods or reasons? Who has any right to make any command or demand upon God? Without such rights, God still meets us at our point of need and invites such a question concerning His son, Israel.

---

[55] c.f. Isaiah, Chapter 5.

> **Isaiah 45:12-13.** *I have made the earth, and created man upon it: I, even my hands, have stretched out the heavens, and all their host have I commanded. [13]I have raised him up in righteousness, and I will direct all his ways: he shall build my city, and he shall let go my captives, not for price nor reward, saith the LORD of hosts.*

This prophesy from God is pointed at the apostate Israel, and reminds the nation that it is He who created all that is, and it is He who has the sole ability to command the heavens and all their hosts. God is the creator and commander of all of the universe and all of eternity. He has the wisdom to command heaven and earth, and has the wisdom to choose how He will redeem Israel. Referring again to Cyrus, God declares His future purpose as, though the nations of Israel and Judah will fall, He will preserve a remnant in Babylon, a remnant that will be given into the hands of Cyrus the king of Persia, who will (1) rebuild the destroyed Jerusalem, and (2) release the captive remnant. Furthermore, Cyrus will do this without any potential of reward, but rather simply because God will lead him to do this.

The proof of prophesy is in its historical fulfillment. Even the name, "Cyrus" is amazing since this prophecy was written 200 years before Cyrus did, indeed conquer the nations, set the remnant of Israel free, and commission and support the rebuilding of Jerusalem. We find much of the history of the rebuilding in the books of Ezra and Nehemiah.

This passage illustrates for us an amazing and true narrative of how God intervenes and works among His people in order to accomplish His purposes. We might ask ourselves, if God can accomplish so much through a pagan named Cyrus, how much can He accomplish when He works through the hearts and the hands of today's faithful believers. It is God's purpose that Israel be saved and be brought back into the fold of the Good Shepherd, the Messiah, Jesus Christ who, as YAHWEH, gave this very message to Isaiah. Christians today carry that message of love and grace and have the opportunity to share it with those who need to hear it, including the prodigal nation of Israel, the blood descendents of Abraham. However, God also opened up His purpose of grace to the Gentiles, who now make up the bulk of the fellowship of faithful believers. God also works through faithful Christians to bring his message of grace to the Gentiles, those who are not blood descendents of Abraham.

Let us be reminded that as God could work through Cyrus, He can also work through the life of every Christian who will fully submit to His Lordship, and by so doing bring under His influence and control all of the gifts, talents, and interests that He has given us. It is then that God can fully use us, and it is then that we will see Him accomplish His purpose through us.

Isaiah 53:1-12.
Prophecies of the Messiah

"Have it your way!" We often have a well-defined model of how we want and expect our world to appear as we interact with it. Those responsible for product sales spare no effort in their attempt to determine what people want and expect from their products in order to maximize profits. Sellers want our expectations satisfied so that we will purchase and re-purchase their products. Skilled merchants understand the basic nature of man, a nature that responds positively when their expectations are realized and negatively when they are not.

We apply this formula when we order food from a restaurant. We have an expectation that is based upon many factors, and when the food arrives, we are free to be critical of its form and content. The writer of the menu attempts to describe the meal in a way that will attract an order and the chef attempts to cook a meal that fulfills the expectation of the customer. If an automobile does not perform to the level of our expectations, we refer to it as a "lemon." If an employee does not perform to the level of our expectations, the employee may be disciplined or fired. If a product does not perform to the level of our expectations, we may return it to the store for a refund. We choose products on a store shelf that appear to most closely meet our expectations for performance and price.

Sometimes our expectations can form a model that is so well-defined that we miss something important when it does not quite match that which we are looking for. A good example is how we often fail to recognize someone we know when we meet them in a context that is radically different from the norm. Sometimes we just can not see things that do not fit nicely into our little box of expectations. How great a part do our expectations play in the way we accept the many things we see and do in this life? Do you set the level of your expectations so high that you are difficult to satisfy? This set of expectations play a large part in defining our world view, the box of rules within which we comfortably live. As long as things fit within that box, we are satisfied, but things that do not fit our little box are rejected, ignored, or all-together missed. When our expectations cause us to be blind to what clearly appears before us, we are experiencing what is referred to by some as "paradigm paralysis," a behavior that is literally dysfunctional.

One area of life where people suffer most from paradigm paralysis is in their recognition of God's grace and His purpose in the salvation of man through faith in Him. God's plan has always been to redeem those who place their faith and trust in Him, a redemption that is provided through the atonement paid by Jesus Christ on the Cross of Calvary. Yet, the expectations that people have concerning God leave many blind to the gospel message. Throughout the history of man, people have tended to create their own gods that fit their own viewpoints concerning the world around them. However, God has revealed Himself to mankind from the very beginning, through the patriarchs such as Adam and Noah, and through the Hebrew lineage of Abraham, Isaac, Israel, etc. He also revealed His purpose through the Hebrew prophets as God chose to bring His redemptive purpose through the house of Abraham. Not only did God reveal His purpose, He also revealed the nature and work of the coming Messiah who would bring to culmination His redemptive work.

If any group of people should have recognized the Messiah, it was the ancient Jews. The prophets had given them many detailed and accurate descriptions of the coming Messiah, suitable for recognizing Him when He came. However, the Jews have given little or no importance to the Messianic testimonies of the patriarchs and prophets, preferring to apply their own interpretation to fit their own model and persecuting those who disagree with it. Instead of looking for a Messiah who would reconcile them to God, they expected a Messiah who would be a worldly king who would defend them from their enemies, and in the time of the first century the Jews thought the Messiah would rise up and defeat the Romans. They could not understand that the scope of the Messiah's victory would be far broader than that of a simple national struggle since they were so obsessed with their worldly political status.

One of the most graphic descriptions of the nature and purpose of the coming Messiah are in four poems, or songs, that Isaiah writes[56] and the following passage is from the last of these.

> **Isaiah 53:1.** *Who hath believed our report? and to whom is the arm of the LORD revealed?*

As we approach Isaiah's Servant Song, we should note that the Hebrew form of poetry is used. Instead of rhyming words, Hebrew poetry rhymes ideas or concepts. Consequently, each idea that is presented is repeated. However, Isaiah takes advantage of this literary form and uses the pair to describe more completely what it is he is presenting. We can see this

---

[56] Isaiah 42:1-4, 49:1-6, 50:4-9, 52:13-53:12.

rhyming in 53:1 as the statement has two similar clauses, the second further illustrating the idea of the first. As this passage is read, pay close attention to the duplicate patterns, as each contributes to our understanding of the author's message.

Isaiah writes his prophecy in the past tense, as if the coming of the messiah had already taken place, painting a historical picture that is vivid and complete. When the Messiah did come, most of the Jews, in particular the Jerusalem leadership, failed to link Jesus with the prophecies that they already knew. Blinded by their well-defined expectations of a kingly and militant leader, they could not believe that Jesus was the Messiah, a disbelief that characterizes Judaism today. The Messiah would appear quite the opposite of everything they were expecting. His appearance was different, and the purpose of the work was different, even though Isaiah and others had provided correct prophecy. Jesus would do a mighty work as He came to save all people from the condemnation of the separation of God that sin engenders in all mankind. To whom was this work (*arm of the LORD*) revealed? We find that those who believed that Jesus is the Messiah were very few: limited to the 12 apostles and at least 150 other disciples who are often mentioned individually and by group throughout the New Testament. How could the entire nation fail to recognize the Messiah who fulfilled all of the prophecies concerning Himself? The answer is the same today: disbelief. The pattern of disbelief has continued through the centuries with very few believing "our report," even today.

> **Isaiah 53:2.** *For he shall grow up before him as a tender plant, and as a root out of a dry ground: he hath no form nor comeliness; and when we shall see him, there is no beauty that we should desire him.*

One area in which our expectations are denied is in Jesus' appearance. God commanded that no "graven image" be made, meaning simply that man is not to make icons to be worshipped. The legalistic Jews over-applied this commandment, decreeing by law that creating images of people, animals, and plants is contrary to the Law. Consequently, though we do have images of others who lived during Jesus' time, we have none of Jesus, Himself. The study of this passage may reveal that those images of Jesus that we have come to accept from artistic interpretation are quite erroneous.

Tender Plant / Root from dry ground. Isaiah describes Jesus' appearance to be quite different than that which we tend to depict today. Movie producers would have a hard time finding an actor to accurately play Jesus, and audiences would be unresponsive because of one simple truth: Jesus was not a physically attractive man. Jesus was raised by Joseph and Mary, and later only by Mary. Jesus' father Joseph was a worker of wood, but we know that he is out of Jesus' life sometime after Jesus became a young man. Jesus was called the "Son of Mary", not the "Son of Joseph," forever impressing the stigma of His status as a fatherless child of Mary. These people were poor, and rejected by society as a whole. So, Jesus grew up poor in a village that was not respected by the surrounding community. A tender plant that grows in dry ground is withered and stressed, and one who grows up poor and rejected shows the signs of such stress. These signs could be clearly seen on Jesus.

What were the Jews expecting for their Messiah? Certainly, this poor, fatherless son of Mary could not be the Messiah. We may be reminded that David also received the same treatment when Samuel came to Eli to anoint the next king.

No Comeliness / No Beauty. It may be noticeable that when artists render their interpretations of the appearance of Jesus, they do so by employing every form of beauty they can capture. Jesus is always depicted as a handsome man who has the physical appearance of that which any culture considers powerful, attractive, and handsome. Isaiah describes Jesus as quite plain, one who would not attract attention based upon his appearance. When the Jerusalem Jews looked upon Jesus they would say, "Certainly this man can be no king" simply because of His lack of beauty. His hair and skin would be dark, a product of His Jewish lineage, and His skin was probably quite rough and mottled both from his mean upbringing and from the stresses of growing up in an arid and sunny region.

Who is "we"? Some discussion has taken place over the years concerning who Isaiah is referring to in this passage, with most agreeing that Isaiah is identifying with his Jewish nations, Israel and Judah, those to whom the prophecy was directly written. Isaiah's definition of "we" can easily be extrapolated to refer to all who have had the opportunity to know who Jesus is and have rejected Him. This would include not only the Jewish descendants who live today, but also those non-Jews who have rejected the gospel. God's Word was not meant for Abraham and his descendents alone, but for all people who, through learning of God's love, would turn to Him in faith.

What were the Jews expecting? Certainly this unattractive, grizzled man could not be the Messiah, the King who would lead them out of bondage. We may recall that Saul was selected as the first King of Israel, and his only asset was his physical appearance.

> **Isaiah 53:3.** *He is despised and rejected of men; a man of sorrows, and acquainted with grief: and we hid as it were our faces from him; he was despised, and we esteemed him not.*

The Jews were looking for a celebrated king, not a fatherless child from a no-account village, or a despised criminal as He appeared on the Cross. Society looked down on Jesus immediately from his birth, referring to Him as the Son of Mary, a constant reminder that he was considered a child who was conceived out of wedlock. Jesus would have faced rejection throughout His entire life, a rejection that was only repeated when He started His redemptive ministry. The Jewish leadership hated Jesus from the very beginning of that ministry when His message did not match their expectations. His message stressed the demonstration of true love over the keeping of Jewish tradition and the law of the scribes. His call for repentance and faith exposed the hypocrisy of the Jerusalem Jews. His rejection of the Jerusalem traditions and His claim to be able to forgive sins brought charges of blasphemy from the Pharisees who quickly came to despise him. As we look at Jesus' ministry we can see the accuracy of Isaiah's prophecy. Jesus was a man of sorrow who grieved over those who rejected God's offer of grace as He watched the Jerusalem Jews turn away from Him and reject Him.

Though Isaiah's description of the Messiah is clear, the Jews still held to the image of a victorious military leader who would restore Israel as a nation. The redemptive ministry of Jesus was not what they were expecting at all.

> **Isaiah 53:4.** *Surely he hath borne our griefs, and carried our sorrows: yet we did esteem him stricken, smitten of God, and afflicted.*

The Jews attributed misfortune, disease, suffering, and grief to the just reward for sin. The smug Jerusalem Jews viewed Jesus' suffering as a just reward for His own sins, never realizing that it was for their own sins that He was crucified. They mocked Him as they crucified Him, as they attributed His pain to God's judgment. They believed that they were righteous because of their adherence to Mosaic Law and the Jewish traditions, failing to recognize that their attempts at keeping the law did not prevent them from continuing in sin, a sin that separates them from God. It is we who deserve separation from God, and it is we who deserve to experience the penalty for our sins. It is our grief and our sorrows that Jesus bore for us.

> **Isaiah 53:5.** *But he was wounded for our transgressions, he was bruised for our iniquities: the chastisement of our peace was upon him; and with his stripes we are healed.*

What was the purpose of the coming of the Messiah? The Jews could never look past their nationalism and see God's true purpose for them. They looked back to the kingdom of David when Israel was free of foreign domination and control, a state that lasted a very short time for the troubled nations of Israel and Judah. They saw the Messiah as the One who would free them from the bondage of foreign domination. However, God's plan was that the Messiah would do far more for the people He loves. He would free them from the bondage that dooms them to eternal separation from God: the bondage of transgression. Transgressions are those sins that we commit by choice, literally in rebellion against God. Iniquities refer to the godless "debauchery," behavior that is the product of unrestrained human nature. It is this sin that separates people from a Holy and Just God. These are also the sins that found no remedy in the sacrificial system of the Old Testament.

Jesus suffered on the cross, shedding His blood when He was brutally scourged, as the one true and final sacrifice so that all who place their faith and trust in God would find forgiveness for those sins. It was for our iniquities and for our transgressions that Jesus was wounded, bruised, and died. The penalty for our sin was placed upon Him, upon Messiah, upon God Himself.

> **Isaiah 53:6.** *All we like sheep have gone astray; we have turned every one to his own way; and the LORD hath laid on him the iniquity of us all.*

The consequence of our paradigm paralysis, our failure to recognize Jesus as the Messiah who came to take away the sins of the world, is to remain in that sin. Ignorant of God's plan of salvation, we seek our own plan of righteousness, wandering in a spiritual wilderness like sheep without a shepherd. Each has made his own choice of who his God is, and like the Israelites of the period of the Judges, each does what is right in his own mind. However, even as we have strayed, the Messiah did come to bring us back home as He took upon Himself the penalty for our sin, a self-sacrifice that we could never make. In this way, the Messiah came to bear the burden of our unrighteousness. That was His prophesied purpose.

> **Isaiah 53:7.** *He was oppressed, and he was afflicted, yet he opened not his mouth: he is brought as a lamb to the slaughter, and as a sheep before her shearers is dumb, so he openeth not his mouth.*

As Isaiah describes the suffering of the Messiah he notes that, like a lamb to the slaughter, he offered no physical or verbal resistance. Where those for whom He died would have responded with violence, Jesus demonstrated a spirit of calm peace. Jesus' treatment at the hands of the Roman guards during His beating that preceded the flogging was particularly brutal. The guards fed off the cries for mercy of those whom they tortured, and Jesus was silent. They went from punching to pulling out His beard in an effort to get Him to cry out. As Jesus, the Messiah and Creator, humbled Himself and endured this treatment at the hands of ungodly men, He knew the purpose of this sacrifice would be to save even those who beat and tortured Him. It was to save the ones who crucified Him. It was to save the ones who despised Him. Jesus went before the Roman crucifixion like a lamb to slaughter, probably praying continually for the physical strength and endurance that would be necessary to take His place on the cross of Calvary.

Some argue that Jesus contradicted this prophecy and demonstrated a point of spiritual weakness when He cried out "My God, My God, why has Thou forsaken me"[57] while He hung, crucified on the cross. However, these are not Jesus' own words of despair ... these are the first words of Psalm 22, a prophecy of the crucifixion. Jesus' quote points out this Psalm of David, a prophecy that graphically describes the details of the crucifixion of the Messiah, illustrating how all of these events are fulfilling the last prophecies of the Messiah's ministry. As for the apparent despair in these words, the Psalm starts with these words of sorrow, but ends with words of victory.

---

[57] Matthew 27:46.

> **Isaiah 53:8.** *He was taken from prison and from judgment: and who shall declare his generation? for he was cut off out of the land of the living: for the transgression of my people was he stricken.*

Isaiah continues to describe Jesus' treatment during His passion. Jesus experienced imprisonment and was taken to His death following His judgment at the hands of the Romans. The Israelites defined themselves by the Land of God's promise, a land that was held through generations. With no future hope, the Jews placed their hope in their ancestry. One of the most grievous travesties would be experienced by one who is killed before he has an opportunity to have children because their ancestral line would be cut off. Isaiah prophesies that the Messiah would be cut off in this way, dying without leaving behind an heir. Again, Isaiah reminds us that this sacrifice was also given by the Messiah for the transgressions of the people.

> **Isaiah 53:9.** *And he made his grave with the wicked, and with the rich in his death; because he had done no violence, neither was any deceit in his mouth.*

Isaiah clearly states the injustice done to the Messiah. How could a king be treated so unjustly? One can understand how the Jews, expecting a victorious military leader who would reign as the new King of a united Israel could not fit the description that Isaiah presented. Their conclusion was simply that Isaiah's prophecy referred to someone other than the Messiah. By discounting Isaiah's words, selecting only those words of scripture that fit their own world view, they missed the Messiah. Jesus' death held a form of irony that could be fulfilled only through the grace and wisdom of God and certainly through nothing man could ever do. Though Jesus had done no wrong, and as much as the Pharisees hated his teachings, Jesus never stated anything that held any form of error or deceit, He was treated as a criminal and crucified in the company of thieves. To the ancient mind, to be found guilty was to be guilty, and to be guilty of anything was to be worthy only of being despised. Hence, being crucified with thieves was to be as a thief, and to be buried in association with the wicked is to be buried with the wicked.

It is unlikely that either of the two thieves were buried in a tomb. Even if their families were rich enough to have a carved-out tomb in which to lay them, the shame that their crucifixion brought upon their families would most likely have cost them that honor. The Hebrew word for evil hell, Gehenna, comes from the name of the place outside the city where the unclaimed dead were piled and burned, the place where the bodies of the two thieves were probably discarded. However, Joseph of Arimathea, a disciple of Jesus, was wealthy and asked that Jesus be buried in his family tomb. In this act, this disciple unwittingly fulfilled Isaiah's prophecy that Jesus would also die with the rich. The Hebrew words that are rendered "made his grave" and "death" refer to the manner of death and the place of burial, respectively, helping us to understand Isaiah's meaning: Jesus' manner of death was shared with thieves, yet his place of burial was among the rich. We might remember again that these words were penned approximately 700 years prior to the crucifixion of Christ (740 - 698 B.C.)

> **Isaiah 53:10-11.** *Yet it pleased the LORD to bruise him; he hath put him to grief: when thou shalt make his soul an offering for sin, he shall see his seed, he shall prolong his days, and the pleasure of the LORD shall prosper in his hand. [11]He shall see of the*

travail of his soul, and shall be satisfied: by his knowledge shall my righteous servant justify many; for he shall bear their iniquities.

The suffering of the Messiah was not without purpose, nor was it contrary to God's plan. God demonstrated through the entire history of man, and most fully through the experience of Israel, that man cannot be made perfect by any manner of his own work. Before man was given the law of Moses, faith was literally impossible to find, with almost every man, like sheep, turning astray. Through Moses, God laid down a model of righteousness, a written illustration of what a righteous person looks like. This model became interpreted as law, and in such was found a law that no person could keep. Given a free choice, people simply cannot live without committing sin, and it is sin that separates man from God. Since man cannot pay the penalty for his own sin, God chose to do it for us. God came down to man to take upon Himself the punishment for our sins when He hung on the cross and became sin, Himself. Though the event was the most dramatic and horrific event in the history of man, Jesus' death paid the sin debt. Jesus paid a debt that He did not owe so that those who place their faith and trust in God will be found righteous. Man could do no work to find righteousness, so that work was done by God.

Though childless, he shall see his seed. Though put to death, he will prolong his days. Though stricken by transgressions, the LORD shall prosper in his work. These are all seeming contradictions that could not be explained except through the atoning death of the Messiah on the Cross of Calvary. Jesus' heirs are all of those who find eternal salvation by placing their faith and trust in God, trusting in God's word that reveals the Savior and Lordship of Jesus. Though He was put to death, He rose again and ascended into Heaven. And though He took on the guilt of transgressions, He did so without sin. These are all prophecies that were fulfilled in Jesus, and only in Jesus.

> **Isaiah 53:12.** *Therefore will I divide him a portion with the great, and he shall divide the spoil with the strong; because he hath poured out his soul unto death: and he was numbered with the transgressors; and he bare the sin of many, and made intercession for the transgressors.*

Jesus' death on the cross had a clear purpose: so that He could make intercession for sinful man. Can someone come to a saving faith in God and reject Jesus' Lordship and Messiahship? Can someone reject the deity of Christ and find saving faith? Both of these are the same question, and the answer is simply, no. Intercession for transgressors is found only in the Messiah: only in Jesus. When one turns to God in faith and trust, one must also trust His Word, or that trust is in vain. His Word became flesh and dwelt among us[58] in the Messiah, Jesus. The sin of man finds forgiveness only in the work that Jesus did on the cross. Sin loses its power to condemn us only when Jesus stands as our intercessor.

Any study of Isaiah's servant songs: the prophecies of the life, ministry, and death of the Messiah, serves to reveal a prophecy that has been entirely, completely, and accurately fulfilled in the life, ministry, and death of Jesus. After Jesus' resurrection and ascension, His identity as the Messiah was fully revealed. The Hebrew Christians no longer called Him Jesus son of Mary, or Jesus son of Joseph. He was now Y'shua Meshia. The Greek form of this name is Jesus Christ.

---

[58] John 1:1-14.

The Jews failed to recognize the true Messiah because they formed another Messiah in their own world view. They could not equate Isaiah's Messiah with the Messiah that they truly wanted, nor the one that Israel is still looking for. They could not rationalize Isaiah's Messiah with any human reason. The same is still true today. Even after 2000 years of evidence, modern Jews still reject Isaiah's prophetic description of Jesus. At the same time, with such a simple plan of grace, Jews and non-Jews alike reject the sacrifice that the Messiah gave at the cross. God Himself, the Creator and Judge, came down from His place in Eternity to indwell the life of a man, Jesus, who went to the cross to pay the penalty for sin for all who would place their faith and trust in Him. Salvation is that simple: it is just a choice to believe in God's Word, and accept God for who He is, both Savior and Lord. Satan believes in God and is forever lost. Satan believes in Jesus and is forever lost. Satan believes in the Holy Spirit and is forever lost. Satan rejects God's Lordship, the Christian embraces it.

Do not let another day pass without knowing for certain that Jesus is your own Lord and Savior. Jesus is the suffering servant of Isaiah's prophesies, but He is also the exalted LORD, and is worthy to be trusted, worthy to be praised, and worthy to be worshipped. Let us praise Him and worship Him together, joint heirs with Him in eternity.

Isaiah 55:1-13.
Priceless Grace

What price will people pay for the peace that comes with the knowledge of one's security? This may sound like a trivial question, but when one considers the hustle-and-bustle that characterizes the people of the world, the impact of this question is far more profound and far-reaching. What do people spend the bulk of their time and energy doing? What is their primary quest?

No degree in sociology is needed to consider these questions. People work though almost any endeavor to obtain some desired level of physical, social, and spiritual security. People work long and hard hours at jobs in order to earn enough money to obtain some desired level of financial security, often working towards a future with a promise of less financial stress. People depend upon one another for some form of social security. We gather in social groups in order to meet our basic needs for social interaction. We also form in our cultures some activity or work that is meant to provide a desired level of spiritual security, positioning ourselves to be acceptable to our God.

Every human culture throughout all of known history has created some form of religion in an effort to obtain some form of spiritual security. Romans, chapter one, teaches that God has revealed His righteousness to all people, and that all people are keenly aware of their own lack of righteousness. God made people in His own image as spiritual beings, giving them this knowledge of Himself, knowledge of His righteousness, and knowledge of the depravity of man's intrinsic spiritual state. Consequently, there is no shortage of methods that people have created to make themselves "right" with God. We might simply refer to these methods as religions.

Religions all have one characteristic in common: they are systems of prescribed behavior that, when obediently followed, are claimed to earn for its subscribers some level of spiritual security. People dedicate their lives to these systems of earned righteousness that may give the practitioners a belief in their own security, but it is a belief that will quickly be replaced with dread when the final judgment reveals these systems lacking in one simple point: eternal security cannot be earned by any work of man, but by the free gift of grace given by God to all who place their faith and trust in Him alone.

If we define religion as a system of works that makes one right with God, Christianity is not a religion. Christianity is a faith. However, the world largely rejects the precept of faith since free righteousness simply makes no sense. After all, do we not have to work for everything we get? The harder we work, the more we get from our work. We are far more comfortable with a rewards-punishment system that rewards us for the good we do, and punishes us for the bad.

Ancient Judaism is an excellent example of a religion. Though the covenant that God made with Abraham, Noah, Moses, and the nation of Israel was a covenant of faith, the nation turned its back on God in an effort to be more like the pagan nations, and their faith gradually changed to a complex and impossible set of rules and regulations that had to be followed in order for its adherents to be considered righteous. Even the impossibility of the law itself proved that righteousness cannot be obtained by law, but the Jews could not see this.

Isaiah brought his prophesy to Israel and Judah during the years surrounding the fall of the northern nation of Israel, a fall that was predicated by their abandoning their faith in God. The southern nation of Judah would also fall for the same reason as they abandoned their trust in God as they attempted to obtain their political and physical security by making alliances with their warring neighbors. Both nations were swept up in those wars and were ultimately destroyed. Only a remnant of faithful Judeans was maintained by Babylon and would later be freed by Babylon's successors, and it was through those few that the small spark of faith was maintained through the years. Isaiah's prophesy is a call for the nations to return to God as he exposed their self-destructive apostasy. He called for their return to faith in God, and described the future day when the Messiah would come. In the following passage Isaiah reminds the sons of Israel of God's original covenant of faith, a covenant through which true righteousness is found.[59]

> **Isaiah 55:1.** *Ho, every one that thirsteth, come ye to the waters, and he that hath no money; come ye, buy, and eat; yea, come, buy wine and milk without money and without price.*

Isaiah describes this quest for righteousness in a metaphor that observes the willingness of those who are hungry and thirsty to pay a great price to have their need satisfied. Every person has a "thirst" for a relationship with God, though in some it may be repressed by adamant anger and/or rebellion. Because of this, Paul writes that "all are without excuse.[60] Just as man

---

[59] Hebrews, Chapter 11.
[60] Romans 1:20.

knows of the existence of a Holy and sinless God, man is aware of his own sinfulness.

Our own human nature demands a reward system that favors good behavior and punishes sinful behavior. The natural way to look at God is to expect the same from Him, to dispense some form of punishment for our sins and reward for our good works. The problem with this logic is simply that God's only and singular punishment for sin is eternal separation from Himself.[61] There is utterly no work that man can do to change God's demand for righteousness. Isaiah is watching his Jewish culture act out a religious frenzy as they are immersed in the sinful acts that are intended to appease the false pagan Canaanite gods. At the same time the Jews hypocritically believe that they are following the tenets of the Mosaic Law which for them defines righteousness. When they fast, they despise those who do not. When they dress in ceremonial clothes, they despise those who do not. They think of themselves as so righteous and clean that they must cleanse themselves if they even touch an individual who is "unrighteous." Their entire world view is wrapped around a system of religion that describes a manner of work that results in righteousness, so they immerse themselves in it in an effort to provide some justification for their true understanding of their own, hidden, black sinfulness.

> **Isaiah 55:2.** *Wherefore do ye spend money for that which is not bread? and your labour for that which satisfieth not? hearken diligently unto me, and eat ye that which is good, and let your soul delight itself in fatness.*

---

[61] Romans 6:23.

Isaiah illustrates an important truth: This hunger for righteousness is not satisfied with any number of works, but instead can be obtained for only free, requiring no work, no price, and no penalty. This is grace. Isaiah understands the concept of grace, God's simple offer of forgiveness is realized by those who will simply place their faith and trust in Him instead of the works of their own hands.

Isaiah's statement points out those who are engaged in the religious frenzy that we see also all around us. We need not look far to observe the huge variety of ways that people express their religion, ranging from conservative piety to radical violence. We see a variety of religious cultures, each with its own set of rules, doctrines, and rites; each designed to transport its obedient adherents to some state of righteousness. Even Christians and Christian denominations can fall into a reward-punishment system and devise a set of do-s and don't-s that place a legalistic burden upon the members. Many are spiritually bullied into believing a rewards-punishment system when they misunderstand many biblical passages that illustrate the consequences of refusing God's call to faith in Him.

> **Revelation 21:7-8.** *He who overcomes will inherit all this, and I will be his God and he will be my son. But the cowardly, the unbelieving, the vile, the murderers, the sexually immoral, those who practice magic arts, the idolaters and all liars--their place will be in the fiery lake of burning sulfur. This is the second death."*

Even the faithful, when they take a good look at their lives find that there are moments of cowardice, doubt, vile behavior, uncontrolled anger, and sexual immorality either in thought or action. Virtually all faithful people practice at some time some forms of idolatry. Consequently, there are some who teach that if you do these things you will be cast into that lake of fire, separated from God for eternity, having lost the salvation that God originally gave to you. This heretical doctrine leaves the believer at the mercy of the church who may then prescribe any manner of repayments to atone for their sins, restoring them to a right relationship with God. This heresy also tends to place on the faithful a burden of guilt that Jesus died on the cross to permanently remove.

Isaiah is asking, "Why do you do this?" "What is the point of all of this religious mumbo-jumbo? Why do you put so much effort into buying something that is not righteousness? Why do you labor so for that which cannot truly satisfy? Listen carefully: embrace that which is true and good, and delight in what can truly bring righteousness."[62]

> **Isaiah 55:3.** *Incline your ear, and come unto me: hear, and your soul shall live; and I will make an everlasting covenant with you, even the sure mercies of David.*

Why is it so hard to listen to and embrace the true covenant that God has made with man? That covenant that was made with David is the same covenant that God made with Abraham, Noah, Moses, and the nation of Israel. It is the same covenant that God has made with man as revealed and fulfilled by His Son, the Messiah, Jesus Christ: place your faith and trust in God and He will be faithful to forgive your sins and cleanse you of unrighteousness.[63] In the Old Testament covenants, God often used the metaphor of the land to illustrate His grace. God simply promised Israel that, if they would place their trust in Him, God would provide them a land and protect them,

---

[62] Author's paraphrase.
[63] 1 John 1:9, et. al.

keeping them with Him. It was when Israel turned their back on God and chased after pagan gods and religious legalism that God removed His hand of protection as both Israel and Judah chose to separate themselves from Him.

An everlasting covenant is one that does not change. God's covenant has never changed. Though we break the Holy Scriptures into an "Old Testament" and a "New Testament", there is no substantial difference in the covenant that is illustrated in them. Jesus fully illustrated the meaning of the covenant, integrating it into all of His teaching, a teaching that is consistent with God's communication to mankind through the prophets as is evident here.

> **Isaiah 55:4-5.** *Behold, I have given him for a witness to the people, a leader and commander to the people. ⁵Behold, thou shalt call a nation that thou knowest not, and nations that knew not thee shall run unto thee because of the LORD thy God, and for the Holy One of Israel; for he hath glorified thee.*

The ancient Jews, and modern man for that fact, had great difficulty in appropriating a world view that was spiritual rather than physical and temporal. They perceived David as a worldly king and Israel as a nation what would someday rule all nations under a new king, a messiah. However, Isaiah reveals a quite different purpose in David, and consequently, the Messiah: a witness, a priest, and an example of faith. The Hebrew words used for these three titles would be controversial to Isaiah's contemporaries who desired a military conqueror. The Jews simply cannot recognize who David really is, and they cannot recognize who the Messiah is. When the very nation of the faithful is formed one day, they will also fail to recognize it, yet this New Israel, this New Jerusalem[64] will draw all nations into itself, not in military conquest, but rather as a refuge for all who place their trust in the LORD, the Holy One of Israel. The Christian church today is fulfilling the evangelistic call that God originally gave to Israel and is illustrated in Isaiah's prophesy. Imagine the impact on the world today if Israel had recognized and embraced Isaiah's prophesy and recognized and embraced his testimony that the Messiah is Jesus Christ. If Israel and all modern Judaism were to place their faith and trust in God, and in Him alone, they would fulfill their calling as a "witness to the people." The leader and commander of Israel would be Jesus Christ, "*Y'shua Meshia*." the Messiah who would, through Israel, show God's grace to the entire world.

> **Isaiah 55:6.** *Seek ye the LORD while he may be found, call ye upon him while he is near:*

The time for faith is now. We only have an opportunity to turn to the LORD during this short life, a time that is just a moment in eternity. We live like we think we will live forever, and we can always put off today what we can do tomorrow, but someday tomorrow will not come, and that someday could be today. To miss out on an eternal relationship with God simply over the desires and greed for today can only be described as foolishness. God is offering forgiveness and restoration without cost to anyone who will simply turn to Him now, while such a choice is still possible. The age of grace began with the creation of man, and will end at one's death, and ultimately at the end of the age of man. With death comes the final judgment, and those found without the mark of faith, the Holy Spirit, will find only eternal separation from,[65] God's plan for those who chose separation from Him in life.

---

[64] Revelation 3:12, et. al.
[65] Revelation, Chapter 20.

How do we turn to God in saving faith?

> **Isaiah 55:7.** *Let the wicked forsake his way, and the unrighteous man his thoughts: and let him return unto the LORD, and he will have mercy upon him; and to our God, for he will abundantly pardon.*

The answer is simply: repentance. Repentance is not feeling sorry or mournful over sin, though sorrow and mourning over sin is certainly an appropriate response to sin. Repentance is the actual act of turning away from that sin. It is a volitional choice to abstain from sinful behavior as one seeks to be obedient to God, who is both Savior and personal LORD. If one rejects the Lordship of God, despising the right that God has to be the One Ruler over us, we have rejected God. In this way, to reject the LORD is to reject God. It is the LORD who created all that is,[66] and He came and dwelt among us in the life of Jesus Christ, the Messiah. Consequently, to reject Jesus is to reject God. Salvation comes by turning from one's wickedness and turning to God in faith.

Do the faithful continue to sin? Yes, they do, but Isaiah states that God will have mercy upon the sinner, and his pardon is abundant. This is simply because once one turns to God in repentance and faith, forgiveness is found. Sin has lost its power to separate the faithful from God any longer.[67] Since sin can no longer condemn, sin will no longer separate one from God. Jesus died to pay the penalty for that sin. Salvation is truly salvation: one is eternally saved.

---

[66] John 1:1-14.
[67] Romans 8:1.

> **Isaiah 55:8.** *For my thoughts are not your thoughts, neither are your ways my ways, saith the LORD.*

The concept of eternal salvation defies all human logic. We are far more comfortable with a rewards-punishment system. However, the truth may be better understood when we understand the LORD. To choose to continue in sin because of the abundance of grace is to deny God's Lordship over oneself,[68] the mark of an unrepentant sinner. We simply cannot put God into a little box that we can all understand, and we cannot ascribe God's plan or thoughts as our own. This is the God who created the universe. Our knowledge is limited to what we have read and heard, and filtered by what we can understand. Our thoughts are riddled with sin and selfishness, greed and envy. This is not the mind of Christ, a mind that is characterized by a love that we simply cannot fully embrace. We try to use the Greek term, agape, to describe the unconditional love that God has for all of His creation, the same love that Christians are also to share unconditionally with all people. As much as we may try, we will never fully understand the thoughts and ways of God. We are simply too blinded by our own immersion in this sinful and pagan world, a world that is shaped by our own human nature, a nature that is quite alien to the nature of God.

> **Isaiah 55:9.** *For as the heavens are higher than the earth, so are my ways higher than your ways, and my thoughts than your thoughts.*

How separated are God's thoughts from our own? I am sometimes amazed at some people who consider themselves

---

[68] Romans 12:1.

so close to God that they share the same thoughts. When someone says, "God told me ..." I would attempt to place them along-side the prophets like Isaiah and Micah, and somehow, they always seem to come up lacking. What I am hearing is truly to be interpreted, "My opinion is ...". We will simply never be "so spiritual" that our thoughts are God's thoughts, though we may in our spiritual pride wish it were so.

How different are our thoughts? Isaiah describes the difference as that of the height of the heavens over that of the earth. This statement implies a mathematical ratio that boggles the human mind to that point that most humans will never consider it, nor would they choose to do so. The distance across our KNOWN universe is about 20 billion light years, and a single light year is about 600,000,000,000,000 (600 million million) miles. Ok, if we divide that distance by the width of the earth, we find that the universe is 1,400,000,000,000,000,000,000 (1.4 sextillion) times larger than the earth. This is the universe that we know of. This could be one of billions of universes that God created. God created all of this for His own pleasure and holds it in the full breadth of its size and age in the "palm of his hand". How big is God? How much greater is He than anything we can imagine? Any real study of the physics of cosmology reveals a true immensity to God's creation that extends far beyond what we observe in our own backyard.

Isaiah uses this difference between the immensity of the universe and what we see in our own backyard as a metaphor for the difference between the ways of God and the ways of man. Like the ants who diligently work in the context of their own little anthill are ignorant of everything they cannot see or perceive, we are also diligently engaged within the context of our little backyard that we can understand. We have no more idea of the true mind of God than the ant does of ours. Again, how big is your God?

> **Isaiah 55:10-11.** *For as the rain cometh down, and the snow from heaven, and returneth not thither, but watereth the earth, and maketh it bring forth and bud, that it may give seed to the sower, and bread to the eater: 11So shall my word be that goeth forth out of my mouth: it shall not return unto me void, but it shall accomplish that which I please, and it shall prosper in the thing whereto I sent it.*

Yet, as separated as our mind is from the true mind of God, unlike the relationship of our mind to that of an ant, God reveals His purpose to us in ways that we can understand. The metaphor that Isaiah uses is that of a gentle rain, or a soft snow that falls gently and nurtures the soil, enabling life. God has revealed Himself through creation in a way that all people can see.[69] He has revealed His plan and His purpose through the patriarchs and prophets of the Old Testament, and He has fully revealed Himself through the Messiah, Jesus Christ. God's Word falls upon us like a gentle rain, or like a soft snow, not like a hurricane or a blizzard. Shakespeare wrote of this in one of his plays, "*The quality of mercy is not strained; it droppeth like a gentle rain from heaven.*"[70] The gospel of Christ is gentle and immersed in God's unconditional love. God's Word empowers eternal life just like the soft rain brings life to the physically living. Just as the living (flowing) water eternally feeds the tree on the riverbank,[71] God's Word will bring forth life in those who receive it. God's Word will not fail. Though many in this world choose to rebel against God and

---
[69] Romans, Chapter 1.
[70] *The Merchant of Venice*, Act IV, Scene II, 1600[A.D.]
[71] Psalm 1:3.

reject this living water, the remnant of the faithful will remain until the end of the age. People will continue to hold true to their faith and pass it on to their children. People will continue to hold true to their faith and share it with others. God's Word will continue to prosper according to His own will. It is His will that none would perish,[72] but in His gentleness it is also His will that people come to him by their own choice.

> **Isaiah 55:12-13.** *For ye shall go out with joy, and be led forth with peace: the mountains and the hills shall break forth before you into singing, and all the trees of the field shall clap their hands. [13]Instead of the thorn shall come up the fir tree, and instead of the brier shall come up the myrtle tree: and it shall be to the LORD for a name, for an everlasting sign that shall not be cut off.*

God calls us to come to Him while He is still near. There is coming a time when this age will come to a close. This will be a time when the Messiah will return in glory, a time when those who have turned to God in faith will be gathered together in a celebration of rejoicing.

Imagine a world that is completely free of the influence of sin. Imagine a world where satan[73] and his demons have been removed, and the black prince of this world is replaced with the glorified Prince of Peace. This is what will take place when the time of grace on this earth comes to an end. Isaiah describes the level of the expression of joy as one that is so pervasive that even the trees of the field will clap their hands. The mountains and the hills will break out in singing praises for the

---

[72] 2 Peter 3:9.
[73] The failure to capitalize the name of satan is both a literary error and a personal choice.

LORD God. The hills and the trees are a testimony to God's creation and to His grace, and even through these He demonstrates His mercy.

All who seek God can find that experience of hand-clapping trees, and the promise of that joy is offered to all who will simply place their faith and trust in God. Salvation is not found by any work of man, a principle that even God opposes because of its penchant for stimulating pride rather than faith.[74] Salvation is offered to all as a free gift of grace, a gift that we do not deserve. Salvation cannot be purchased for any price, yet people still try to pay for that which God offers for free. There is nothing to compare to God's grace.

While we are yet living a life that is immersed in sin, a life that is characterized by sinful actions and sinful thoughts, God has provided a plan for our salvation. The Messiah came, fulfilled the revelation of God to man, and suffered on the cross, so that those who place their faith and trust in Him can be set free from the burden, guilt, and condemnation of sin. Jesus paid the price for that sin, a price we cannot pay, so that we who do not deserve salvation can find it. This is grace. How can we reject the Creator who loves us so? As you consider the unfathomable love of God and the grace that He has offered, look into your own heart and seek out your true response to His Lordship. Is God truly your Lord, or are you holding back part of this sinful world from Him, holding onto ungodly attitudes and actions that are separating you from the joy and peace that comes with forgiveness? Come to God while He is near, and He will carry you the rest of the way home. That is grace: full, saving, and free.

---

[74] Ephesians 2:9.

Isaiah 58:1-14.
Time Out!

Exhaustion. There are few who are not quite familiar with the term. As we find ourselves at the beginning of the 21st century we are surrounded with technology that was undreamed of only a few years ago. We have gadgets and machines that perform virtually all of the mundane tasks that were commonly the most burdensome a century ago. For example, fasting was an important part of ancient custom simply because the preparation of meals took from one-quarter to one-half of the workday. By a century ago that number settled down to about one-quarter. Today, with fast food restaurants, microwave ovens, and numerous other kitchen gadgets and food preparation methodologies, food preparation time has been drastically reduced. Almost every act of labor has been touched by technology, resulting in faster and more efficient production. With so much time saved through the application of modern technology, the most vexing problem of modern society should be the determination of how to spend all this leisure time that technology has created.

Quite the opposite is true. As technology has allowed people to do more things more quickly, people have chosen to do more things. As production levels increase, the stress to maintain that production increases. If we can make 10,000 products per day, why not 12,000? The 40-hour work week is only a memory for salaried workers who often work 60 hours per week or more for the same compensation that is provided at 40. We try to fit into our frenetic schedules all those activities that we deem necessary like one would place pieces into a jigsaw puzzle. Never in the history of man have so many people been found taking drugs to help them cope with the pace of today's culture. The pace of today's culture affects more people physically than ever before, dramatically increasing the incidences of almost every stress-related illness known.

Can things get worse? Can the pace get faster? The answer to that question is an obvious, "yes" since the factors that promote this frenzy still rule the day. Technology continues to create more products that increase efficiency and productivity. The drive to increase production still continues. For those caught up in this upward spiral of activity, there is one simple future: the years will pass, opportunities for experiencing the really important things in life will be bypassed, and death's door will be found far too soon.

This is not the "abundant life" that God promises to those who place their faith and trust in Him (John 10:10). That abundant life is offered, but we push it out of the way in our drive to accomplish the tasks of this age while largely ignoring God's Word and the voice of the Holy Spirit as He whispers through the deafening blast of each day's activity.

As we participate in the activities of each day, are we really accomplishing what is best for us, relationally, physically, and spiritually? That is, are we nullifying the opportunity to develop relationships with those we love as we work to "provide" for them? Are we damaging the "temple of the Holy Spirit" by our lifestyle? Are we damaging or even nullifying our relationship to God by filling our time with works that are not profitable for our spiritual life or for the kingdom of God?

> **Isaiah 58:1.** *Cry aloud, spare not, lift up thy voice like a trumpet, and show my people their transgression, and the house of Jacob their sins.*

The pace of life in ancient Israel and Judah had become frenetic in many of the ways that ours has, but for different reasons. The religious traditions that surrounded the Mosaic Law had placed so many requirements on people that many, in an effort to obtain righteousness, were immersed in its authority as it dictated many of the actions of each day. At the same time the people had forgotten the purpose of the law, ignoring its author, the LORD. Instead of living a life of faith that results in godly living, they ignored faith and tried to live by a law that describes godly living. This godless approach to righteousness enabled them to follow after the sensual pagan gods of the Canaanites. They ended up adding the ungodly pagan practices to their daily regimen, creating conflicts of purpose and allegiance that were complex and spiritually debilitating.

God called upon Isaiah to lift up his voice "like a trumpet" and expose the sin of the people. He was to "spare not," to make use of every resource to expose every sin without compromise. The metaphor of the trumpet is used to represent something that is loud and clear. Isaiah's call to the people is to be both loud and clear so that all will hear God's message: a message that would show the people the nature of their transgressions and sins: their errors of "missing the intended mark," and their volitional sins of choice. Under the traditional Mosaic system of sacrifice, the former sins were atoned for by applying various types of sacrifices. There was no sacrifice for the latter form of sin. The people had committed both.

The sin of Israel and Judah was their choice to follow after the secular and pagan culture rather than to place their faith and trust in God. They claimed that God is their LORD, but they did not live out what they testified. Their days were not characterized by prayer and seeking God. Instead, God was placed out-of-sight and out-of-mind while the "more important" activities of every day were exercised.

Not much has changed. Certainly we can easily argue that the secular and pagan people of the world today live like this. However, Isaiah's prophecy is not intended for the lost. His prophecy is intended for those who claim the name of the LORD. This message is for those who claim to place their trust in the LORD but have placed Him out-of-sight and out-of-mind for most, if not all, of the day. This message is for most Christians today. If this is true, is it any wonder that many Christians do not experience the joy, peace, and love that characterizes the "abundant life" that Jesus promises? It is time for someone to shout loudly and clearly to the church today. The church needs to be lifted out of its immersion in this pagan society.

> **Isaiah 58:2.** *Yet they seek me daily, and delight to know my ways, as a nation that did righteousness, and forsook not the ordinance of their God: they ask of me the ordinances of justice; they take delight in approaching to God.*

Again, Isaiah is presenting his prophecy to those who claim the name of the LORD. This is a very religious people. Their activity is, by their own design, intended to seek God. Calling themselves the "Children of God," they look back at their history as they proudly declare that theirs is the nation that is righteous. Unlike their pagan neighbors they look to their rites and sacrifices, the observance of their celebrations and to their Mosaic Law, and see among these the fruit of their righteousness. They pray with grand words, and make a great spectacle of their worship of God. They wear their religion like a badge of pride. This is an apt description of religious zealotry, but is religion the answer to righteousness? Does God look upon their rites and sacrifices and their robes and sackcloth as the foundation of their righteousness?

Security in the LORD is found only when one places their faith and trust in Him. Security is not found in religion, nor in religious piety or practice. Religion is a work that man can perform, and no work leads to salvation. The ancient Jews were willing to characterize the work of their lives in their attempt for righteousness. However, such work only results in exhaustion, not peace. Joy is not found when the Holy Spirit is not part of the heart. This is evident in the true fruit of their labor.

> **Isaiah 58:3.** *Wherefore have we fasted, say they, and thou seest not? wherefore have we afflicted our soul, and thou takest no knowledge? Behold, in the day of your fast ye find pleasure, and exact all your labours.*

The idea behind fasting is simple: much of the daily routine was devoted to the preparation and consumption of food. The Mosaic Law called for only one day of fasting: the day of Atonement, Yom Kippur, on the 10th day of the 7th month. This fast was accomplished by the abstinence of both food and drink for one day: a time measured from sunrise to sunset. This allowed the entire day to be devoted to prayer while the

High Priest entered the Holy of Holies in the center of the Tabernacle/Temple to offer the sacrifice of atonement of the people's transgressions. Fasting was intended to be motivated by the mourning that accompanies the realization of one's responsibilities for their own sin. Two other ceremonial fasts were established in early Judaism, the "Seventeenth Day of Tammuz" to remember the 586 BC siege of Jerusalem, and the "Ninth Day of Av," to commemorate the destruction of the Jewish temples (586 BC, 70AD.) These ceremonial fasts set the pattern for a culture of fasting in response to times of great sorrow. For example, King David fasted in grief as Bathsheba's son lay dying (2 Sam. 12:16).[75]

The foundation and purpose of fasting was clearly established to allow people to bring their personal focus upon God. However, by the time Isaiah writes, Israel had removed God from its religion. Fasting was a legalistic enterprise that focused attention on the one fasting rather than on the One for whom fasting was intended. Fasting became a badge of righteousness rather than a cause for expressing sorrow or repentance. Fasting became so shallow and ritualized that the First-Century orthodoxy fasted on regular Mondays and Tuesdays. (Note orthodox fasting did not preclude eating, drinking, and working during hours of darkness.) For this reason Christians were encouraged to fast, but to do so on Wednesdays and Fridays so that their true fasting would not be confused with orthodox hypocrisy (from the *Didache*).[76]

This important religious practice had lost its purpose and its power. When they fasted they realized no spiritual fruit at all. They came to declare fasting as a great affliction as they

---

[75] Ziglar, Toby. (Winter, 1999) First-Century Fasting. Biblical Illustrator (25:2). Pg. 73

[76] Yechiel, Eckstein, Rabbi. (1984). What Christians Should Know About Jews and Judaism. Waco TX: Word Books. pg. 143-145.

denied themselves (for 12 hours!). The only reward they found in fasting was found by massaging their own pride and ego as they made a great deal about how they suffered so. Those who fast would put on a countenance of suffering, as they try to draw attention to their own piety.

> **Isaiah 58:4.** *Behold, ye fast for strife and debate, and to smite with the fist of wickedness: ye shall not fast as ye do this day, to make your voice to be heard on high.*

God does not reward rites and rituals with any form of His approval. The original point of fasting was for the purpose of prayer. Fasting had become a religious rite that the continued to perform while their heart was immersed in wickedness. Isaiah points out that rather than taking time out (fasting) for prayer, they are far more willing to take time out to engage in ungodly behaviors such as fighting with those whom they disagree (strife), verbally and physically persecuting those who expose or reject their hypocrisy (debate), even to the point of murder (smite with the fist of wickedness.)

Is it any wonder their religion has no power? It may be easy to point fingers at the apostate nations of Israel and Judah, but when we look at our own lives, though we may not have a culture of fasting, do we take time out for prayer? Would we rather spend our "spare" time seeking God, or seeking the 18th hole? One does not need to set aside eating, drinking and working from sunrise to sunset in order to be righteous. One only needs to turn from the frenetic pace of the day and calmly turn to God in prayer. It is far easier to hear the leading of the Holy Spirit when one is quietly focused on the LORD than when one is immersed in the noise and distraction of daily routines, whether they be secular (as is the state for modern Christianity) or religious (as it was for ancient Israel.)

Isaiah 58:5. *Is it such a fast that I have chosen? a day for a man to afflict his soul? is it to bow down his head as a bulrush, and to spread sackcloth and ashes under him? wilt thou call this a fast, and an acceptable day to the LORD?*

Fasting was a common rite among the ancient near-eastern cultures. This was not a new practice when God instituted its use on the Day of Atonement. The fast was established as a "time-out," a time when one could turn from the cares of normal daily activities and seek the LORD in a spirit of repentance and praise. It was not intended to be an affliction on the people as the Jews had come to ascribe. Again, even the hypocrisy of their afflicted state is exposed when we realize they only fasted during daylight hours. Though the mournfulness that accompanies true repentance is a part of the product of the true purpose for fasting, it is not intended to bring attention to the worshipper, but rather to God. It is not appropriate that one who is fasting would, instead of turning to God in prayer, turn to the public with his "head in a bulrush," an idiom for the physical expression of great sadness. Though we come to God in repentance, He has forgiven the sin of those who have placed their faith in Him, so there is no need for great sadness, and there is particularly no need to express that sadness before people. Some would stick their head in the bulrushes so far that they would dress up in sackcloth (black mourning clothes) and sit in cold ashes, tossing the ashes up in the air, covering themselves as an expression of profound mourning. This great show was not intended to come to the LORD in sincerity, but rather to demonstrate their self-professed righteousness to the public.

For them, personal faith in God had been replaced by a religion. Judaism had become an exclusive club with a God-theme. Is it possible that there are church fellowships today that are more characterized as a Christian club than a body of faithful believers? Churches can become a social club with a God-theme when they go through the rites of the practice of their worship without the power of the Holy Spirit. To these, "going to church" is an affliction, like fasting was an affliction to the ancient Jews. These find any excuse to stay home during worship times, and they watch their timepieces during the services because their heart is not there, but outside the walls of the facility. We should not be too quick to criticize the hypocritical practices of the ancient Jews when we may be doing some of these same things ourselves.

> **Isaiah 58:6-7.** *Is not this the fast that I have chosen? to loose the bands of wickedness, to undo the heavy burdens, and to let the oppressed go free, and that ye break every yoke? ⁷Is it not to deal thy bread to the hungry, and that thou bring the poor that are cast out to thy house? when thou seest the naked, that thou cover him; and that thou hide not thyself from thine own flesh?*

What would happen if we chose to actually implement spiritual fasting in our lives. True, spiritual fasting involves taking a time-out from our daily regimen so that we can focus specifically on prayer, read and meditate on scripture, and seek the LORD's will and purpose in our lives. Isaiah points out some of the products of the practice of true fasting:

1. Loose the bands of wickedness. Immersed in a pagan and secular world, Christians are constantly touched by its wickedness. Without a concerted effort to make consistently godly choices, one can be easily swept up by the world-view of this secular world. Without a time-out we can become insensitive to the Holy Spirit, and begin accepting falsehood as truth, and begin accepting ungodly opinions as normative. When we take some quality time to listen to the LORD and study His word, the wickedness of this world loses its brutal hold.

2. Undo the heavy burdens, letting the oppressed go free, breaking every yoke. Much of the stress we experience in this world comes from the way we embrace burden. We think that we must fix everything. We hold on to anger and bitterness that pulls us down. We hold grudges against others that weigh us down. These are all burdens that we do not have to carry. Quality time with the LORD will reveal where we are angry, bitter, or holding grudges and through prayer it is possible to turn those over the LORD when we recognize that these are ungodly attitudes that need to be set down.

It is common knowledge that if one places a frog in hot water, it will jump out. However, if one places the frog in cold water that is slowly raised in temperature, the frog will not notice, and will die when the water is too hot for the frog to handle. It is easy for us to fall into this same situation as we are exposed to an ungodly world. Little by little we accept its secular views until there is little that separates us from evil.

3. Deal thy bread to the hungry. Another part of immersion in the secular is to forget the call upon every Christian to share God's love with others. We can be so caught up in taking care of ourselves that we neglect those around us who need help. The more secular we become, the more finite becomes the type of person we are willing to associate with. We find that we must step out of our "comfort zone" in order to minister to others when that zone has become constrictively small.

Disassociation with others can lead to prejudice, and prejudice to bigotry. Our world becomes defined by our own backyard, and we look down on anything that is different. When we take time out for the LORD, our selfishness and sin can be exposed, and our prejudices can be turned over to the LORD. God has called all Christians to love all people, and this clear truth can be heard when we take time to listen. Instead of turning our backs on those who are a little different, and those who are in need, one can look for opportunities to share God's love. When this is done, the walls of ignorance that separate us from those God has called us to minister will fall.

> **Isaiah 58:8-9.** *Then shall thy light break forth as the morning, and thine health shall spring forth speedily: and thy righteousness shall go before thee; the glory of the LORD shall be thy reward. ⁹Then shalt thou call, and the LORD shall answer; thou shalt cry, and he shall say, Here I am. If thou take away from the midst of thee the yoke, the putting forth of the finger, and speaking vanity;*

Isaiah then goes on to note what happens when our prideful self-will is replaced with obedience to the LORD. The darkness of the sins and burdens is replaced with the light of God's love as it both shines on the one who is faithful and shines through him/her. This is true righteousness. Righteousness is not found in a obedience to a law or religious rite. It is found by submitting to the LORD in faith. The prayers of the unrighteous are certainly heard by an omniscient God, but their self-centeredness is not in agreement with His will. Sin separates us from God, and repentance restores that relationship. When we take a time-out to sincerely seek the LORD, we will find Him close by.

Isaiah 58:10-12. *And if thou draw out thy soul to the hungry, and satisfy the afflicted soul; then shall thy light rise in obscurity, and thy darkness be as the noonday: [11]And the LORD shall guide thee continually, and satisfy thy soul in drought, and make fat thy bones: and thou shalt be like a watered garden, and like a spring of water, whose waters fail not. [12]And they that shall be of thee shall build the old waste places: thou shalt raise up the foundations of many generations; and thou shalt be called, The repairer of the breach, The restorer of paths to dwell in.*

The primary motive of the self-righteous ancient Jew that is described in the earlier verses is to gain the attention and respect of others. They strove to wear the religious garb, speak the religious language, and follow the religious practices. However, because their actions were solely for show, the LORD would not honor their actions. Isaiah points out, however, when one demonstrates true righteousness, the fruit of that love of others is spontaneous, and does not take place without notice, and not without blessing. Many have had the opportunity to experience traveling to a foreign country, or to a distant location, to take part in a missionary effort. These may include rebuilding storm-ravaged homes, or feeding those who have just experienced disaster. It may be bringing food or medical aid to war- or economically-torn areas. Without fail, the result of these efforts upon the giver is two-fold. First, the experience destroys the walls of ignorance that separates us, and second, the giver ends up experiencing as much blessing as those to whom the ministry was given. Those engaged in mission may come home exhausted, but they also come home strengthened and encouraged spiritually. Many who return from a true mission experience want to turn around and go back.

Isaiah describes this result, and also points out that the minister will be called "the repairer of the breach," an idiom for one that brings others closer to God. All the attention that the unrighteous faster was attempting to attain only exposed his own hypocrisy as people see through his self-centeredness and the wickedness of his true nature. However, no such wickedness is seen in the life of the sincere minister of the LORD, and his works are seen as bringing the love of God to others. Where the first one desires the attention and notoriety, the second has no such desire. However, the works of both are seen. The first is seen as a hypocrite, the second as a minister of the LORD. The first finds his religion a burden, and the second finds his faith a joy. The first finds exhaustion, and the second finds renewed strength. The first is the fasting of man, the second is the fasting that God intended: taking time out to seek His will.

> **Isaiah 58:13-14.** *If thou turn away thy foot from the sabbath, from doing thy pleasure on my holy day; and call the sabbath a delight, the holy of the LORD, honourable; and shalt honour him, not doing thine own ways, nor finding thine own pleasure, nor speaking thine own words: [14]Then shalt thou delight thyself in the LORD; and I will cause thee to ride upon the high places of the earth, and feed thee with the heritage of Jacob thy father: for the mouth of the LORD hath spoken it.*

Up to this point in this chapter, Isaiah has been referring to works of righteousness. Though the example used is that of fasting, its meaning goes beyond that one religious act as he is referring to all of the works that we do. As this chapter closes, Isaiah also brings attention to the practice of worship. Just as the secularization of the body of Christ has affected its works, it has also affected its worship. Having spent over thirty years "leading worship" the one issue that I have found universal is that real worship rarely happens. When people come to the worship "service" they are usually not interested in their true worship of the LORD. Instead, they are distracted by every secular sin that they bring with them, whether it be anger and bitterness toward one another, displeasure with the songs selected, displeasure with the sermon, or the pastor's inattention to the clock. We look at each other rather than at the LORD. We evaluate the music, evaluate the sermon, rather than evaluate our own need for repentance. Instead of searching our own hearts, we attempt to criticize that of others. Some approach worship in a manner similar to the ancient Jews, who made loud and boisterous prayers as they attempted to bring attention to their own righteousness. Some seem to forget that Jesus is the LORD of the church and choose to usurp that position for themselves, demanding that others accede to their demands.

When we approach worship in this same selfish way the result of the experience is not exactly what God intended. However, when we turn aside our own selfish desires and approach worship in true love of the LORD, God promises that this Sabbath will be a delight. Like fasting, the concept of the Sabbath is to take a break, a time-out from our daily routine so that we can focus on the Lord. Note that Isaiah describes true worship as not of our own ways, and own pleasure, and not of the speaking of our own words. Worship is all about honoring God, not ourselves or each other.

Some who have had the opportunity to experience a situation where true worship was experienced refer to it as a "mountain top" experience. It is God's will that all worship be such an experience. It is only when we let our own unrepented sin stand between us and the LORD is our worship experience compromised.

As Isaiah was exposing the secularization of the Jewish religion, he also exposes to us the secularization of modern Christianity. The ancient Jews failed to experience the power of the Holy Spirit in their religious experience, and many Christians today profess the same. Some denominations have come to the point that the preaching of the gospel has been replaced by the preaching of secular philosophy. The church has come to embrace the same ungodly practices of the secular world in which it is immersed as its membership has exchanged true worship of the LORD with a social experience.

It may be time for the church to take a close look at Isaiah's prophecy, as he accurately described the secular nature of the Jews. It is time for every individual to take time out and examine their own heart, whether it be a time of fasting, or a time of worship. Upon examination, has your love of the LORD been usurped by your love of this life? Has worship of the LORD been replaced with religious practice? God promises abundant blessings for those who will return to the original form of fasting and Sabbath: to take time out and sincerely seek the heart of God.

Bibliography

_____, The Breath of Yahweh Scorching, Confounding, Anointing: The Message of Isaiah 40-42. *Journal of Pentecostal Theology*, 5 no 11 Dec 1997, p 3-34.

Abma, Richtsje. Travelling from Babylon to Zion: Location and Its Function in Isaiah 49-55. *Journal for the Study of the Old Testament*, 22 no 74 Jun 1997, p 3-28.

Adamthwaite, Murray R. Isaiah 7:16: key to the Immanuel prophecy. *The Reformed Theological Review*, 59 no 2 Aug 2000, p 65-83.

Albertz, Rainer. Darius in place of Cyrus: the first edition of Deutero-Isaiah (Isaiah 40.1-52.12) in 521 BCE. *Journal for the Study of the Old Testament*, 27 no 3 Mar 2003, p 371-383.

Ashdown, Shelley. A cognitive semantic approach to redeemer (Gō'ēl) in Deutero-Isaiah. *Acta Theologica*, 35 no 1 2015, p 10-36.

Balentine, Samuel E. Isaiah 45: God's 'I Am,' Israel's 'You Are'. Horizons in Biblical Theology, 16 no 2 Dec 1994, p 103-120.

Baltzer, Klaus. The Book of Isaiah. *Harvard Theological Review*, 103 no 3 Jul 2010, p 261-270.

Barram, Michael D. Between Text and Sermon: Isaiah 58:1-12. *Interpretation*, 69 no 4 Oct 2015, p 460-462.

Barré, Michael L. Textual and Rhetorical-critical Observations on the Last Servant Song (Isaiah 52:13-53:12). *The Catholic Biblical Quarterly*, 62 no 1 Jan 2000, p 1-27.

Bartelt, Andrew H. Isaiah 6: from translation to proclamation. *Concordia Journal*, 39 no 1 Wint 2013, p 15-24.

Beuken, Wim. The king diseased and healed (Isaiah 38), the king embarrassed and comforted (Isaiah 39): what do these figures add to the king beleaguered and rescued (Isaiah 36-37). *Ephemerides theologicae Lovanienses*, 86 no 4 Dec 2010, p 379-391.

Beuken, Wim. The manifestation of Yahweh and the Commission of Isaiah: Isaiah 6 read against the background of Isaiah 1. *Calvin Theological Journal*, 39 no 1 Apr 2004, p 72-87.

Beuken, Wim; Doyle, Brian (Translator). Women and the Spirit, the Ox and the Ass: The First Binders of the Booklet Isaiah 28-32. *Ephemerides theologicae Lovanienses*, 74 no 1 Apr 1998, p 5-26.

Biddle, Mark E. Teaching Isaiah today. *Perspectives in Religious Studies*, 36 no 3 Fall 2009, p 257-272.

Bingham, Dwight Jeffrey. Justin and Isaiah 53. *Vigiliae christianae*, 54 no 3 2000, p 248-261.

Bird, Michael F. 'A light to the nations' (Isaiah 42:6 and 49:6): intertextuality and mission theology in the early church. *The Reformed Theological Review*, 65 no 3 Dec 2006, p 122-131.

Blenkinsopp, Joseph. Judah's Covenant with Death (Isaiah XXVIII 14-22). *Vetus testamentum*, 50 no 4 2000, p 472-483.

Blenkinsopp, Joseph. The Sacrificial Life and Death of the Servant (Isaiah 52:13-53:12). *Vetus testamentum*, 66 no 1 2016, p 1-14.

Bosma, Carl J. The challenges of reading the 'gospel' of Isaiah for preaching. *Calvin Theological Journal*, 39 no 1 Apr 2004, p 11-53.

Breytenbach, Cilliers. The Septuagint version of Isaiah 53 and the early Christian formula 'he was delivered for our trespasses'. *Novum testamentum*, 51 no 4 2009, p 339-351.

Cardoso Pereira, Nancy. My people shall be as a tree: forests, labour and idols in Isaiah 44. *The Ecumenical Review*, 59 no 1 Jan 2007, p 68-76.

Carr, William W Jr. Will just any 'God' do?: Isaiah's answer for the question of theological pluralism. *Concordia Journal*, 39 no 1 Wint 2013, p 34-45.

Ceresko, Anthony R. The Rhetorical Strategy of the Fourth Servant Song (Isaiah 52:13-53:12): Poetry and the Exodus-New Exodus.The *Catholic Biblical Quarterly*, 56 no 1 Jan 1994, p 42-55.

Chaney, Marvin L. Whose sour grapes?: the addressees of Isaiah 5:1-7 in the light of political economySemeia, 87 1999, p 105-122.

Clements, Ronald E. Isaiah: a book without an ending? *Journal for the Study of the Old Testament*, 26 no 3 Mar 2002, p 109-126. Publication

Cody, Aelred. A palindrome in Isaiah 40:4b: allowing restoration of an original reading. The *Catholic Biblical Quarterly*, 66 no 4 Oct 2004, p 551-560.

Craigen, Trevor. Isaiah 40-48: a sermonic challenge to open theism. The *Master's Seminary Journal*, 12 no 2 Fall 2001, p 167-177.

Dekker, Jaap. The High and Lofty One Dwelling in the Heights and with his Servants: Intertextual Connections of Theological Significance between Isaiah 6, 53 and 57. *Journal for the Study of the Old Testament*, 41 no 4 2017, p 475-491.

Devanesan, J Christopher Samuel. Sin and colour: a critical evaluation of the western scholarly exegesis of Isaiah 1:18. *Black Theology*, 2 no 2 Jul 2004, p 188-194.

Draper, Jonathan A. What did Isaiah see?: angelic theophany in the tomb in John 20:11-18. *Neotestamentica*, 36 no 1 - 2 2002, p 63-76.

Dunston, Robert (Spring 2009). Isaiah, Micah. *Adult Commentary* 2(3). Nashville, TN: Lifeway Christian Resources. p. 10-101.

Eslinger, Lyle M. The infinite in a finite organical perception (Isaiah vi 1-5). *Vetus testamentum*, 45 no 2 Apr 1995, p 145-173.

Feinberg, Charles Lee. The virgin birth and Isaiah 7:14. *The Master's Seminary Journal*, 22 no 1 Spr 2011, p 11-17.

Fried, Lisbeth S. Cyrus the messiah?: The historical background to Isaiah 45:1. *Harvard Theological Review*, 95 no 4 Oct 2002, p 373-393.

Giere, Samuel D. 'It shall not return to me empty' (Isaiah 55:11): interpreting Scripture in Christ for proclamation. *Currents in Theology and Mission*, 41 no 5 Oct 2014, p 326-339.

Goldingay, John. Isaiah 53 in the pulpit. *Perspectives in Religious Studies*, 35 no 2 Sum 2008, p 147-153.

Goldingay, John. Isaiah Then and Now: Reflections on the Responses to The Theology of the Book of Isaiah. *Journal of Pentecostal Theology*, 25 no 1 2016, p 30-42.

Goswell, Gregory Ross. The literary logic and meaning of Isaiah 38. *Journal for the Study of the Old Testament,* 39 no 2 Dec 2014, p 165-186.

Grillo, Jennie. 'From a Far Country': Daniel in Isaiah's Babylon. *Journal of Biblical Literature*, 136 no 2 2017, p 363-380.

Grisanti, Michael A. Israel's Mission to the Nations in Isaiah 40-55: An Update. *The Master's Seminary Journal*, 9 no 1 Spr 1998, p 39-61.

Grogan, Geoffrey W. (1986). Isaiah. *The Expositor's Bible Commentary*. Vol. 6. Grand Rapids, MI: Zondervan Publishing House.

Hayes, Katherine M. 'A spirit of deep sleep': divinely induced delusion and wisdom in Isaiah 1-39. *The Catholic Biblical Quarterly*, 74 no 1 Jan 2012, p 39-54.

Hays, Christopher B. The covenant with Mut: a new interpretation of Isaiah 28:1-22. *Vetus testamentum*, 60 no 2 2010, p 212-240.

Hays, Rebecca Whitten Poe. Sing me a parable of Zion: Isaiah's vineyard (5:1-7) and its relation to the 'Daughter Zion' tradition. *Journal of Biblical Literature*, 135 no 4 2016, p 743-761.

Hochberg, Shifra. Isaiah 40 and Donne's 'A valediction: forbidding mourning': a case for possible influence. *Christianity and Literature*, 63 no 3 Spr 2014, p 325-335.

Isbell, Charles D. The limmûdîm in the Book of Isaiah. *Journal for the Study of the Old Testament*, 34 no 1 Sep 2009, p 99-109.

Jones, John Davis. Churches of Christ and Isaiah 7:14. *Restoration Quarterly*, 59 no 3 2017, p 175-182.

Jong, Matthijs J de. A note on the meaning of beṣædæq in Isaiah 42,6 and 45,13. *Zeitschrift für die alttestamentliche Wissenschaft*, 123 no 2 2011, p 257-262.

Keiser, Thomas A. The Song of Moses a basis for Isaiah's prophecy. *Vetus testamentum*, 55 no 4 2005, p 486-500.

Kennedy, James M. Yahweh's strongman?: the characterization of Hezekiah in the book of Isaiah. *Perspectives in Religious Studies*, 31 no 4 Wint 2004, p 383-397.

Kim, Hyun Chul Paul. An Intertextual Reading of 'A Crushed Reed' and 'A Dim Wick' in Isaiah 42.3. *Journal for the Study of the Old Testament*, 24 no 83 Jun 1999, p 113-124.

Klangwiesan, Yael. 'Camelot': the paradox of Zion in Isaiah. *Colloquium*, 40 no 1 May 2008, p 38-53.

Konkel, August H. The sources of the story of Hezekiah in the book of Isaiah. *Vetus testamentum,* 43 no 4 Oct 1993, p 462-482.

Landy, Francis. I and eye in Isaiah, or gazing at the invisible. *Journal of Biblical Literature,* 131 no 1 2012, p 85-97.

Landy, Francis. Prophecy as a trap: Isaiah 6 and its permutations. *Studia theologica*, 69 no 1 2015, p 74-91.

Landy, Francis. Strategies of Concentration and Diffusion in Isaiah 6. *Biblical Interpretation*, 7 no 1 Jan 1999, p 58-86.

Landy, Francis. Torah and anti-Torah: Isaiah 2:2-4 and 1:10-26. *Biblical Interpretation*, 11 no 3 - 4 2003, p 317-334.

Landy, Francis. Vision and Voice in Isaiah. *Journal for the Study of the Old Testament*, 25 no 88 Jun 2000, p 19-36.

Lane, Harry A. (Spring, 2009). The Syro-Ephraimitic War. *Biblical Illustrator* 35(3). Nashville, TN: Lifeway Christian Resources. p. 64-67.

Lessing, Robert Reed. Isaiah's servants in chapters 40-55: clearing up the confusion. *Concordia Journal*, 37 no 2 Spr 2011, p 130-134.

Lessing, Robert Reed. Preaching from Isaiah 56-66. *Concordia Journal*, 39 no 1 Wint 2013, p 46-54.

Lessing, Robert Reed. Translating instantaneous perfect verbs: interpreting Isaiah 40-55. *Concordia Journal*, 38 no 2 Spr 2012, p 134-140.

Lessing, Robert Reed. Yahweh versus Marduk: creation theology in Isaiah 40-55. *Concordia Journal*, 36 no 3 Sum 2010, p 234-244.

Lindblad, Ulrika Margareta. A note on the nameless servant in Isaiah xlii 1-4. *Vetus testamentum*, 43 no 1 Jan 1993, p 115-119.

Lyons, Michael A. Psalm 22 and the 'Servants' of Isaiah 54; 56-66. *The Catholic Biblical Quarterly*, 77 no 4 Oct 2015, p 640-656.

Mason, Steven D. Another flood?: Genesis 9 and Isaiah's broken eternal covenant. *Journal for the Study of the Old Testament*, 32 no 2 Dec 2007, p 177-198.

Mastnjak, Nathan. Judah's covenant with Assyria in Isaiah 28. *Vetus testamentum*, 64 no 3 2014, p 465-483.

McInnes, Jim. A methodological reflection on unified readings of Isaiah. *Colloquium*, 42 no 1 May 2010, p 67-84.

Menzies, Glen W. To What Does Faith Lead? The Two-Stranded Textual Tradition of Isaiah 7.9b. *Journal for the Study of the Old Testament*, 23 no 80 Sep 1998, p 111-128.

Mitchell, Christine Karen. A note on the creation formula in Zechariah 12:1-8; Isaiah 42:5-6; and Old Persian inscriptions.*Journal of Biblical Literature*, 133 no 2 2014, p 305-308.

Moore, R. Kelvin. (Spring, 2009). The Political Climate for Isaiah & Micah. *Biblical Illustrator* 35(3). Nashville, TN: Lifeway Christian Resources. p. 43-46.

Moyise, Steve. Jesus and Isaiah. *Neotestamentica*, 43 no 2 2009, p 249-270.

Nogalski, James. Changing Perspectives in Isaiah 40-55. *Perspectives in Religious Studies*, 43 no 2 Sum 2016, p 215-225.

Noonan, Benjamin J. Zion's foundation: the meaning of boḥan in Isaiah 28,16. *Zeitschrift für die alttestamentliche Wissenschaft*, 125 no 2 2013, p 314-319.

Olley, John W. 'No Peace' in a Book of Consolation: A Framework for the Book of Isaiah? *Vetus testamentum*, 49 no 3 Jul 1999, p 351-370.

Olyan, Saul M. Is Isaiah 40-55 really monotheistic? *Journal of Ancient Near Eastern Religions*, 12 no 2 2012, p 190-201.

Oosting, Reinoud. The counsellors of the Lord in Isaiah 40-55: a proposal to understand their role in the literary composition. *Journal for the Study of the Old Testament*, 32 no 3 Mar 2008, p 353-382.

Paganini, Simone. Who speaks in Isaiah 55.1?: notes on the communicative structure in Isaiah 55. *Journal for the Study of the Old Testament*, 30 no 1 Sep 2005, p 83-92.

Press, Michael. 'Where are the gods of Hamath?' (2 kings 18.34 & Isaiah 36.19): the use of foreign deities in the Rabshakeh's speech. *Journal for the Study of the Old Testament*, 40 no 2 Dec 2015, p 201-223.

Raabe, Paul R. Christ and the nations: Isaiah's Gentile oracles. *Concordia Journal*, 39 no 1 Wint 2013, p 25-33.

Rhodea, Greg. Did Matthew conceive a virgin?: Isaiah 7:14 and the birth of Jesus. *Journal of the Evangelical Theological Society*, 56 no 1 Mar 2013, p 63-77.

Roberts, J J M. Security and justice in Isaiah. *Stone-Campbell Journal*, 13 no 1 Spr 2010, p 71-79.

Rudman, Dominic. Midrash in the Isaiah Apocalypse. *Zeitschrift für die alttestamentliche Wissenschaft*, 112 no 3 2000, p 404-408.

Schipper, Jeremy. Interpreting the lamb imagery in Isaiah 53. *Journal of Biblical Literature*, 132 no 2 2013, p 315-325.

Schipper, Jeremy. Why does imagery of disability include healing in Isaiah? *Journal for the Study of the Old Testament*, 39 no 3 Mar 2015, p 319-333.

Seitz, Christopher R. A palindrome in Isaiah 40:4b: allowing restoration of an original reading 'You are my servant, you are the Israel in whom I will be glorified': the servant songs and the effect of literary context in Isaiah. *Calvin Theological Journal*, 39 no 1 Apr 2004, p 117-134.

Seitz, Christopher R. How Is the Prophet Isaiah Present in the Latter Half of the Book? The Logic of Chapters 40-66 within the Book of Isaiah. *Journal of Biblical Literature*, 115 no 2 Sum 1996, p 219-240.

Seufert, Matthew. Reading Isaiah 40:1-11 in light of Isaiah 36-37. *Journal of the Evangelical Theological Society*, 58 no 2 Jun 2015, p 269-281.

Sherwin, Simon J. In search of trees: Isaiah XLIV 14 and its implications. *Vetus testamentum*, 53 no 4 2003, p 514-529.

Sloane, Andrew. Justice and the atonement in the Book of Isaiah. *Trinity Journal*, 34 no 1 Spr 2013, p 3-16.

Smith, Gary V. Isaiah 40-55: which audience was addressed?. *Journal of the Evangelical Theological Society*, 54 no 4 Dec 2011, p 701-713.

Stone, Bebb Wheeler. Second Isaiah: Prophet to Patriarchy. *Journal for the Study of the Old Testament*, 17 no 56 Dec 1992, p 85-99.

Sweeney, Marvin A. Micah's debate with Isaiah. *Journal for the Study of the Old Testament*, 25 no 93 Jun 2001, p 111-124.

Tiemeyer, Lena-Sofia. The watchman metaphor in Isaiah lvi-lxvi. *Vetus testamentum*, 55 no 3 2005, p 378-400.

Troxel, Ronald L. Isaiah 7,14-16 through the eyes of the Septuagint. *Ephemerides theologicae Lovanienses*, 79 no 1 Apr 2003, p 1-22.

Van Winkle, D W. Proselytes in Isaiah XL-LV? A Study of Isaiah XLIV 1-5. *Vetus testamentum,* 47 no 3 Jul 1997, p 341-359.

Viezel, Eran. A note to vy'zkhv (Isaiah 5,2). *Zeitschrift für die alttestamentliche Wissenschaft,* 123 no 4 2011, p 604-607.

Walton, John H. The imagery of the substitute king ritual in Isaiah's fourth servant song. *Journal of Biblical Literature,* 122 no 4 Wint 2003, p 734-743.

Watts, John D.W. (1985). Isaiah 1-33. *Word Biblical Commentary* Vol. 24. Waco TX: Word Books.

Watts, Rikki E. Echoes from the past: Israel's ancient traditions and the destiny of the nations in Isaiah 40-55. *Journal for the Study of the Old Testament,* 28 no 4 Jun 2004, p 481-508.

Wegner, Paul D. How many virgin births are in the Bible? (Isaiah 7:14): a prophetic pattern approach. *Journal of the Evangelical Theological Society,* 54 no 3 Sep 2011, p 467-484.

Wenkel, David H. Wild beasts in the prophecy of Isaiah: the loss of dominion and its renewal through Israel as the new humanity. *Journal of Theological Interpretation,* 5 no 2 Fall 2011, p 251-263.

Wilson, Ian Douglas. Yahweh's Consciousness: Isaiah 40-48 and Ancient Judean Historical Thought. *Vetus testamentum,* 66 no 4 2016, p 646-661.

Wong, Gordon C I. Faith in the present form of Isaiah vii 1-17. *Vetus testamentum,* 51 no 4 2001, p 535-547.

Woude, Annemarieke van der. Can Zion do without the servant in Isaiah 40-55? *Calvin Theological Journal,* 39 no 1 Apr 2004, p 109-116.

Yechiel, Eckstein, Rabbi. (1984). What Christians Should Know About Jews and Judaism. Waco TX: Word Books. pg. 143-145.

Ziglar, Toby. (Winter, 1999) First-Century Fasting. *Biblical Illustrator* (25:2). Pg. 73

Printed in Great Britain
by Amazon